Bradley's Moral Psychology

Don MacNiven

Volume 3
Studies in the History of Philosophy

The Edwin Mellen Press
Lewiston/Queenston

Library of Congress Cataloging-in-Publication Data

MacNiven, Don.
  Bradley's moral psychology.

  (Studies in the history of philosophy ; v. 3)
  Bibliography: p.
  Includes index.
  1. Bradley, F.H. (Francis Herbert), 1846-1924.   2. Ethics, Modern--20th
century.   I. Title.   II. Series: Studies in the history of philosophy
(Lewiston, N.Y.) ; v. 3.
  B1618.B74M33   1987   171'.3   87-1731
  ISBN 0-88946-306-9 (alk. paper)

This is volume 3 in the continuing series
Studies in the History of Philosophy
Volume 3 ISBN 0-88946-306-9
SHP Series ISBN 0-88946-300-X

The Edwin Mellen Press   The Edwin Mellen Press
P.O. Box 450   P.O. Box 67
Lewiston, New York   Queenston, Ontario
USA 14092   CANADA L0S 1L0

Printed in the United States of America

For Elina and Maia,

who matter most.

ACKNOWLEDGEMENT

Parts of chapters 1, 2 and 3 have previously appeared in an article entitled "Bradley's Critiques of Utilitarian and Kantian Ethics," _Idealistic Studies_, (XIV, No. 1. January, 1984), pp. 67-83. I thank the editor for giving me permission to use this material.

CONTENTS

PREFACE

F. H. Bradley has been until very recently a neglected philosopher. The only major work of his which remained in print was Ethical Studies, but even this has been withdrawn. The historical explanation for this neglect by English-speaking philosophers is thought to be easily found (Passmore, A Hundred Years of Philosophy, 1957, and A. M. Quinton, "Absolute Idealism," British Academy, 1971). Bradley was a leading exponent of English Idealism and that philosophical movement expired with the rise of analytic philosophy in this century. Idealism having ceased to be an influential intellectual movement, interest in Bradley's philosophical work also ceased. Bradley was a victim of the revolution in philosophy, led by the Cambridge philosophers G. E. Moore and Bertrand Russell, which occurred at the beginning of this century. The result of the revolution was that philosophy became analytic, academic, and empirical, rather than metaphysical, popular, and apriori. It now concerned itself primarily with detailed analysis of the meanings of words and not with the general nature of thought and reality, or with the great scientific, moral, political, aesthetic, and religious questions of the day. Idealism is looked on as a brief and unfortunate foreign interlude in the empirical tradition of English philosophy which has its roots in the work of Bacon, Hobbes, Locke, and Hume. Both the dates and reasons for the ascendancy of neo-Hegelianism are considered to be precisely known. The period of ascendancy lasted from 1874 (the year which saw the publication of William Wallace's The Logic of Hegel, T. H. Green's edition of Hume's Works, and Bradley's Presuppositions of Critical History) to 1903 (the year that saw the publication of

Russell's _Principles of Mathematics_, and Moore's _Principia Ethica_). The movement started earlier and took some time to become entrenched in the English-speaking universities. The beginning was marked by the publication of Stirling's _The Secret of Hegel_, in 1865. Idealism remained institutionally entrenched in British and North American universities until around 1925 when it began to lose its control. By 1946 it was pretty well finished. During the period 1903-1946 idealism was only a philosophical corpse kept alive by the artificial machinery of academic power. It was brain-dead and by 1946 it was time to be merciful and pull the plug.

The reasons for the introduction of Hegelianism into Britain in the late 19th century, and for its rapid institutionalization in Britain and North America, are also thought to be perfectly clear. Idealism was introduced to Britain, and spread to North America, to arrest the progress of atheistic materialism. The Christian Faith was being undermined by empirical science. Traditional morality and civic virtue were being destroyed by the invidious doctrine of Laissez-faire which had become dominant in morals, politics, economics, and education. The doctrine of Laissez-faire held that unbridled competition between self-interested individuals was the path to all human progress. Philosophy was to become the defender of the faith and the protector of orthodoxy against the radical individualism of utilitarians like Bentham and Mill and social Darwinists like Spenser. Hegel's philosophy with its organic concept of the state, its bias against individualism, its anti-materialism, and evolutionary flavour, seemed perfect for the job.

As Anthony Manser has shown, this "official" story of the rise and fall of English Idealism is inadequate in several ways (Manser, _Bradley's Logic_, 1983). In the first place, the concerns of the idealists were philosophical as well as ideological. They were intellectually dissatisfied with the current empiricist theories of meaning and with their accounts of the logic of scientific and moral reasoning. In the second place, it was the idealists who professionalized philosophy in Britain and not the analysts. They were not, however, narrow professionalists concerned only with standards of competence for their discipline. They were also concerned with the beneficial social purpose their profession served. They wanted to protect the search for and the understanding of truth, which are fundamental values of the practise of philosophizing (see MacNiven, MacEwen, Paiva, "A Code of Ethics for Canadian Philosophers--A Working Paper," Dialogue, 1986). To achieve their goal it was necessary to institutionalize freedom of inquiry to protect philosophy from religious dogmatism. There are other deficiencies in the official story which are also important. For instance, it can be shown that idealism has its native, as well as its foreign, roots and that idealism was in the British air, well before the publication of Stirling's The Secret of Hegel. But for this brief preface it is sufficient to point out that the "official" story is clearly wrong in suggesting that the sole purpose of introducing Kant and Hegel to Britain was to protect orthodox religion and morals.

The story does contain a partial truth. The idealists were concerned about the fate of morality and religion. Most were religious, in the broadest sense of the term, and many were practising Christians. But they were equally concerned about moral and scientific progress. Their social philosophies were, like Bradley's, more progressive than reactionary. Their philosophies were certainly never dogmatic, were always based on reason, and never merely on revelation. Idealism was not a rationalization of moral and religious beliefs dogmatically held, but a genuine and, as I shall try to show, for F. H. Bradley, at least, an important philosophical response to the apparent conflict between science, morality, and religion.

This book has deep personal philosophical significance for me. I was first attracted to the study of philosophy in the late 1950s by the lectures of A. R. C. Duncan, the Scottish idealist who was then chairman of the Department of Philosophy at Queen's University in Kingston. My idealism was softened at Queen's by Martyn Estall of the philosophy department and Julien Blackburn, who was chairman of the department of psychology. The former taught me to respect empiricism and utilitarianism and the latter to respect the achievements of empirical psychology. Still I was convinced that only an idealist approach to ethics, epistemology and metaphysics would ensure philosophical progress, and I am convinced now of the same truth. My studies in Oxford, in the 1960s, at first led me to doubt this but in the long run they have supported it. I now think, though I cannot demonstrate it here, that the later philosophy of Wittgenstein points ultimately to a renaissance of English idealism, especially in its Bradlean form. It is a renaissance that Wittgenstein and many of his disciples would not necessarily be happy with or approve of. Nevertheless it is necessary if philosophy is to progress and if the profession is to keep its obligation to the pursuit and understanding of truth. This book, I hope, will contribute, in its own small way, to that renaissance, which is already well underway (Manser and Stock, The Philosophy of F. H. Bradley, Oxford, 1984).

Parts of Chapters 1, 2 and 3 appeared as an article, "Bradley's Critiques of Utilitarian and Kantian Ethics"

(<u>Idealistic Studies</u>, Volume XIV, no. 1, January, 1984), and I'd like to thank the editor, W. E. Wright, for permission to integrate this material into this book.

Don MacNiven
York University, Toronto
August, 1986

It is this sort of infinite which the mind is. The simplest symbol of it is the circle, the line which returns into itself, not the straight line produced indefinitely; and the readiest way to find it is to consider the satisfaction of desire.

F. H. Bradley. Ethical Studies, p. 78.

CHAPTER I
Ethics and Psychology

Throughout his ethical writings, F. H. Bradley assumed that both science and metaphysics were relevant for ethics. This is an assumption which is not widely shared by contemporary English speaking moral philosophers. Any attempt to derive ethical conclusions from non-moral premises is considered a logical mistake. To base ethics on science or metaphysics is to commit the naturalistic fallacy or to break Hume's "no ought from is" rule. In his critique of metaphysical ethics in Principia Ethica, G. E. Moore argued that all ethical systems based on metaphysical claims were invalid because they presupposed that ethical truths followed from metaphysical truths:

> They all imply, and many of them expressly hold, that ethical truths follow logically from metaphysical truths--that Ethics should be based on Metaphysics.[1]

To try to derive ethical truths from metaphysical truths is to commit the naturalistic fallacy or break Hume's "no is from ought" rule:

> To hold that from any proposition asserting 'Reality is of this nature' we can infer, or obtain confirmation for, any proposition asserting 'This is good in itself' is to commit the naturalistic fallacy.[2]

The only difference between scientific and metaphysical moralists, is that the former try to infer moral conclusions from truths about the natural world, while the latter try to infer them from truths about a supersensible or non-natural world. But whether they start from empirical or a priori truths, the mistake is the same. Bradley certainly appears to break the "no ought from is" rule. He says:

> How can it be proved that self-realization is the end? There is only one way to do that. This is to know what we mean when we say _self_, and _real_, and _realize_, and _end_; and to know that is to have something like a system of metaphysics, and to say it would be to establish that system.[3]

If Bradley's ethics is to have more than historical interest for the contemporary English-speaking philosopher, something needs to be said in defense of the assumption that ethics can be based on science or metaphysics. What, then, is the Naturalistic Fallacy? Simply put, it is this. Nearly all systems of morality begin with, or are founded on, some basic non-moral premises. These could be claims about the nature of man (psychological claims) or claims about the mores of certain societies (sociological claims), or claims about the meanings of moral words (linguistic or semantic claims), or claims about the nature of or existence of God (metaphysical claims). They then proceed from the truth of these non-moral premises to derive moral conclusions, claims about what is good or evil, or what people ought or ought not to do. By simple inspection it can be shown that these arguments are unsound. Let's look at a common example, frequently discussed in recent moral philosophy, the classical defense of hedonism found in the writings of Eudoxus. Aristotle gives the following version of Eudoxus' argument:

> Eudoxus thought pleasure was the good because he saw all things, both rational and irrational, aiming at it, and because in all things that which is the object of choice is what is excellent, and that which is most the object of choice the greatest good; thus the fact that all things moved towards the same object indicated that this was for all things the chief good (for each thing, he argued, finds its own good, as it finds its own nourishment); and that which is good for all things and at which all aim was the good.[4]

Reduced to its simplest form Eudoxus' argument says since everyone pursues pleasure (or believes that pleasure is a good) then everyone ought to pursue pleasure (or pleasure really is a good, something worth pursuing). From a psychological premise Eudoxus had deduced the moral prescription "everyone ought to pursue pleasure." The argument is invalid, because it does not follow that since everyone pursues pleasure everyone ought to pursue pleasure. Just because more women are having abortions to-day does not make abortion morally right. The argument can be made valid by adding the extra, but dubious, moral premise, "we ought to do what everyone in fact does." However the argument now ceases to be a simple deduction from fact to value because a value now appears in the major premise. The same problem occurs in John Stuart Mill's famous defense of the principle of utility in <u>Utilitarianism</u>:

> The only proof capable of being given that a thing is visible, is that people actually see it. The only proof that a sound is audible, is that people hear it; and so for the other sources of our experience. In like manner, I apprehend, the sole evidence it is possible to produce that anything is desirable, is that people do actually desire it. If the end which the utilitarian doctrine proposes to itself were not, in theory and practise, acknowledged to be an end, nothing could ever convince any person that it was so. No reason can be given why the general happiness is desirable, except that each person, so far as he believes it to be attainable, desires his own happiness. This however being a fact, we have not only all the proof which the case admits of, but all which it is possible to require, that happiness is a good: that each person's happiness is a good to that person, and the general happiness therefore, a good to the aggregate of all persons. Happiness has made out its title as one of the ends of conduct, and consequently one of the criteria of morality.[5]

In this much discussed passage, Mill seems to be saying, since people do desire happiness (or pleasure and the absence of pain), therefore people ought to desire happiness (or pleasure and the absence of pain). Eudoxus all over again. G. E. Moore claimed that Mill's argument contains as naive and artless an expression of the naturalistic fallacy as one would wish to find.[6] The mistake is so obvious that Moore wondered how anyone could have missed it. Presumably Mill's argument, like Eudoxus', could be made valid by adding the suppressed premise, "one ought to desire what everyone in fact desires," but again the argument would cease to be a straight deduction from fact to value. Well, why did Mill make such an obvious mistake? Moore's explanation is that the unnoticed transition from 'is' to 'ought' is made possible by Mill's careless use of language in the analogy he draws between sensing and desiring:

> He has attempted to establish the identity of the good with the desired, by confusing the proper sense of 'desirable,' in which it denotes that which it is good to desire, with the sense it would bear if it were analogous to such words as 'visible.'[7]

Mill, according to Moore, commits the fallacy of equivocation, and this in turn enables him to accept an empirical definition of the value word "desirable." For Mill "the desirable," what is worthy of desire or what is good-in-itself, comes to mean "the desired." He is then able to pass over this bridge from fact to value, from what everyone in fact desires, to what they ought to desire, without noticing his mistake. But once the equivocation is seen, the bridge collapses, because the definition has not been justified.

In attempting to show how moral conclusions can be derived from factual premises, Mill transformed ethics into an elaborate but inadequate system of deductive reasoning. The whole programme was, according to Moore, doomed from the start, because it placed Mill on the horns of a dilemma from which there was no escape. As Moore argued, if Mill turned his basic moral principle into a definition of the word "good," all he would be doing when he claimed that "Pleasure is the sole good" was uttering the trivial tautology, "Pleasure is the sole pleasure," rather than a substantial moral principle.[8] Further, Mill's tautology has unacceptable consequences. If it is accepted, it would follow that claims like "Pleasure is not the sole good," would become self-contradictory, meaningless, or analytically false, just as their contradictories would be meaningful, consistent, and analytically true. Normally, Moore pointed out, we do not consider statements like "Pleasure is not the sole good" to be analytically false, because we can meaningfully dispute statements like "Pleasure is the sole good." Moral principles are synthetic and not analytic. So Mill is faced with a choice either of making a significant moral claim, or of putting forward a trivial and unacceptable tautology. If he chooses the former, his fundamental moral principle has not been rationally defended. If he chooses the latter, he would be making a linguistic mistake of some sort, by confusing analytic and synthetic principles, which in turn leads him to make an error in deductive logic and commit the naturalistic fallacy.

Bradley, according to Moore, is making a similar mistake and is faced with the same dilemma as Mill.

Bradley also appears to argue from the fact that everyone can only realize self to the moral claim, everyone ought to realize self, or that self-realization is the end for man. And Bradley has the same unhappy choice as Mill. He must assert either an undefended moral claim or a trivial tautology. But to say that "self-realization is the end for man, is analytically or necessarily true" is not defensible. For we can meaningfully dispute the claim that "self-realization is the sole good," its contradictory, "self-realization is not the sole good," is clearly not analytically false or meaningless. So Bradley, like Mill, is left with either a false linguistic claim, or an undefended moral principle.

Whether we examine the standard criticisms of Eudoxus' defense of hedonism, or Moore's criticisms of Mill's defense of the principle of utility and Bradley's defense of the principle of self-realization, it is clear that the naturalistic fallacy can be understood as a mistake in deductive logic. Hence one way to formulate it is: No set of non-moral premises can entail a moral conclusion. The naturalistic fallacy would be committed by any argument which breaks this rule.[9] The rule is thought in turn to be based on the more general logical principle of tautologies, i.e., that a valid argument cannot proceed from premises to some new affirmation not contained implicitly, in the premises. This would imply that moral claims are distinct from scientific or metaphysical claims, something which both utilitarians and idealists appear to ignore. They both fail to recognize that moral claims are prescriptive; they tell us to make something the case, while scientific and metaphysical claims are descriptive; they tell us what is the case.[10]

If the naturalistic fallacy is interpreted as a mistake in deductive logic then it would not be a valid criticism of non-deductive defenses of moral principles. If it can be shown that a scientific or metaphysical defense of a moral conclusion is a non-deductive argument then it would not be an instance of the naturalistic fallacy. Are Eudoxus' defense of hedonism, Mill's of utility, and Bradley's of self-realization, deductive or non-deductive arguments? Eudoxus' defense of hedonism is clearly deductive. He did break "the no ought from is rule" and Moore's attack would be effective against him. But with Mill and Bradley the situation is radically different. To assess the validity of the anti-naturalists' criticism of them, it will be useful to examine the logical structure of the arguments they used to defend the principles of utility and self-realization, in some detail, and then compare them. I shall deal with Mill's arguments first, then Bradley's.

Any really sympathetic reading of Mill's proof of the principle of utility in <u>Utilitarianism</u> should make it clear that Mill is presenting an inductive argument which appeals to what he believes are the well-established findings of scientific psychology, rather than a deductive one, from fact to value.[11] The title of the chapter in which the proof is given, "Of What Sort of Proof the Principle of Utility is Susceptible," alone should warn the reader that more is going on than the presentation of a simple deductive proof of the principle of utility. Mill is obviously concerned to explain the kind or type of proof that ethical first principles admit of, as well as providing that proof. Hence he says in the paragraph immediately preceding the proof:

> The utilitarian doctrine is that happiness is desirable, and the only thing desirable as an end; all other things

being only desirable as a means to that
end. What ought to be required of this
doctrine, what conditions is it requisite
that the doctrine should fulfill--to make
good its claim to be believed?[12]

It would be relatively safe to assume that whatever
type of proof Mill would opt for it would not likely have
been a purely deductive one. Mill was the most radical
of the British empiricists and although he did not think
deductive arguments were entirely useless, he never considered them capable of providing, by themselves, any
real advance in knowledge.[13] This is true in spite of
Mill's concessions to deductive reasoning as a necessary
component of scientific methodology.[14] The role Mill
assigns to deductive reasoning in scientific method is
considerable, surprising for someone so convinced of the
fundamental importance of inductive reasoning in science.
Mill has often been criticized for not paying sufficient
attention to the role of the a priori in scientific
reasoning. Mill's contemporary William Whewell continually attacked him for ignoring the importance of the
a priori in scientific discovery.[15] In this Whewell, and
critics who followed him, are partly mistaken. For Mill
universal propositions had a significant methodological
role to play in scientific reasoning:

> Induction, therefore, always presupposed,
> not only that necessary observations are
> made with the necessary accuracy, but
> also that the results of these obser-
> vations are, so far as is practicable,
> connected together by general descrip-
> tion. . . ."[16]

The a priori has a methodological, but not an epistemological, role to play in scientific reasoning. Mill's attitude toward deductive reasoning was ambivalent. On the one hand he wanted to argue that deductive reasoning, which goes from the universal to the particular, never produced new knowledge. It was thus less important as a method for establishing truth than inductive reasoning, which goes from the particular to the universal, and always produces new knowledge. On the other hand he wanted to argue that it had a useful role to play in scientific reasoning.

Mill's attitude towards deductive reasoning was controlled by two considerations. The first was his belief that syllogistic reasoning, which for Mill represented deductive reasoning, could never arrive at new truths. Since it was tautological no real inferences could occur in it. The second was his loyalty to his father's radical political philosophy which employed an essentially deductive method to defend representative democracy.[17] These two interests pulled Mill's thought in opposite directions.

Mill's analysis of deductive reasoning was based on the distinction he drew between real and apparent inference.[18] In the argument "all men are mortal because no man is exempt from death," the inference is apparent because the conclusion contains no new truth. Nothing is said in the conclusion which was not already asserted in the premise.[19] Mill thought that syllogistic reasoning suffered from the same weakness, that it too could never arrive at new truths.[20] The conclusion of a valid syllogism cannot contain anything not known, or assumed to be true, in the premises. Syllogistic reasoning cannot produce truth because the truth of the conclusion is already presupposed in the premises.[21] So if we argue that Socrates is mortal because all men are mortal and Socrates is a man, we have learned nothing. Accepting this analysis of the syllogism left Mill with the puzzle of how deductive argument could have any meaningful role in reasoning. Mill's explanation was that the real inference had already taken place in the generalization which produced the major premise, 'all men are mortal.' For Mill all real inference was from particular to particular and hence universal propositions could be epistemologically dispensed with.[22] The general propositions used in deductive reasoning are only records of previous generalizations which are necessary in guiding our thinking through complicated theoretical chains of reasoning. Deductive reasoning was methodologically, but not epistemologically, necessary for science.[23]

Mill's solution to the problem of deductive reasoning, although interesting, is deceptive. What he has really done is to reduce deductive arguments to a form of reasoning in which the only real inferences are inductive. So any inference which occurs in deductive reasoning would not be valid until the induction on which it was based was justified. In the end all real inference for Mill is inductive.[24] Mill's final position in the logic is that all relevant evidence must be provided by the senses. Logic, for Mill, was concerned with inferred truth, which presupposes that some truths had already been established with certainty prior to any reasoning. These certain truths were for Mill the primitive data of consciousness, i.e., our bodily sensations and feelings. Sentences like "I'm hungry now" or "I was vexed yesterday," express true propositions which are simply presented to us in experience. They are propositions whose truth, Mill believed, we cannot doubt. All knowledge, then, is either of this primitive kind or conclusions

inferred from it. All sound arguments are in the end
based on inductions and all real inference is from
particular to particular. Universal propositions can
always be epistemologically dispensed with, even if they
are necessary, as an aid, in scientific reasoning.

Having adopted a radical form of empiricism, it
would be reasonable to assume that the first principle of
morality must be based on the same primitive data. If it
could not it would never be given a rational foundation.
The only alternative is to base our moral claims on
self-evident moral truths. However, according to Mill,
appeals to self-evident moral truths are not arguments at
all. When properly understood they can be shown to be
disguised appeals to personal moral bias. Intuitionism
was, for Mill, the greatest intellectual impediment to
social reform and human progress in his day. In a famous
passage in his Autobiography he cites it as a major
source of support for bad social institutions:

> The notion that truths external to the
> mind may be known by intuition or con-
> sciousness, independently of observation
> and experience, is, I am persuaded in
> these times, the great intellectual
> support of false doctrines and bad insti-
> tutions. By the aid of this theory,
> every inveterate belief and every intense
> feeling, of which the origin is not
> remembered, is enabled to disperse with
> the obligation of justifying itself by
> reason, and is erected into its own
> all-sufficient voucher and justification.
> There never was such an instrument

devised for consecrating all deep-seated
prejudices.[25]

Given this attitude towards deductive systems of
morality, and deductivism in general, it might be expected that he would opt for an inductive defense of the
principle of utility. One modelled along the lines he
developed to defend the empirical method in scientific
reasoning in his System of Logic. The defense would be
similar but not identical, because Mill recognized that
the first principles of morality presented special diffi-
culties. They were intimately related to practise in a
way the first principles of science are not. The results
of moral enquiries are normally expressed in the imperative rather than the indicative mood, hence they tell us
what ought to be the case rather than what is the case:

> Now the imperative mood is the charac-
> teristic of art, as distinguished from
> science. Whatever speaks in rules or
> percepts, not in assertions respecting
> matters of fact, is art: and ethics or
> morality, is properly a portion of the
> art corresponding to the sciences of
> human nature.[26]

Mill recognized that there is an important distinction to be drawn between statements of fact and
evaluations. Statements of fact tell us what is the
case, evaluations tell us what ought to be the case:

> Propositions of science assert a matter
> of fact; an existence, a coexistence, a
> succession, or a resemblance. The

> propositions now spoken of do not assert
> that anything is, but enjoin or recommend
> that something should be. They are a
> class by themselves. A proposition of
> which the predicate is expressed by the
> words ought or should be, is generically
> different from one which is expressed by
> is or will be.[27]

Moral propositions are essentially prescriptive. They are used to guide conduct, not to tell us about the nature of things. This being so, it will not be possible to pass, in a straight deductive way, from fact to value, e.g., from a developed scientific psychology to moral conclusions. The relation between psychology and morality is more complex than this. Of course it is true that we can show, within reason, that a particular action will produce, or will probably produce, a certain balance of pleasure over pain for everyone affected by it. Mill recognized that questions of instrumental value are basically factual. But what cannot be derived from experience in the normal scientific way is confirmation that pleasure, or happiness, are worth pursuing as life goals. Questions of instrumental value are essentially scientific questions. But what of questions of intrinsic value, of the ultimate ends of human conduct? These, according to Mill, cannot be settled by the normal methods of science:

> But though the reasonings which connect
> the end or purpose of every art with its
> means belongs to the domain of science,
> the definition of the end itself belongs

exclusively to art, and forms its pecu-
liar province.[28]

Every practical activity has at least one general
premise not borrowed from science, which asserts that the
end aimed at possesses intrinsic value. In fact, Mill
argues, we really need one ultimate practical principle
on which to base consistent practise. In utilitarian
theory this ultimate practical principle is that happiness or pleasure is the sole end worth pursuing for its
own sake. It is this claim that Mill's famous proof of
utility in Utilitarianism is concerned with.[29] In order
to get general assent for the claim that pleasure or
happiness is the sole end worth pursuing, all anyone can
do is present some general considerations about the
desires and behaviour of mankind which would make the
principle acceptable to reasonable people. Just as the
only reasonable test for showing that something is
capable of being seen is the empirical test of seeing it,
so, analogically, the only reasonable test for showing
that some goal is desirable, is the fact that people
actually desire it for its own sake. To formulate the
ultimate goals of conduct or public policy we need to
start with the actual desires of mankind. One cannot
expect reasonable people to accept the general happiness
as a goal if it is completely unrelated to their actual
desires. Clearly many people do desire pleasure, or
happiness, hence the principle of utility has made out
its claim to be one of the ends of conduct and also a
criterion of morality. But further, not only is pleasure
or happiness one of the ends of conduct, it is the only
end of conduct. If this more radical claim can be
established then Mill will have shown, to his

satisfaction, that pleasure or happiness is the sole good and thus the only criterion of morality.

The remainder of Mill's proof is used to establish this controversial thesis, something Mill recognized as difficult to achieve.[30] The doctrine of psychological egoism (human beings can only pursue their own pleasure) is easily falsified by experience because people pursue other ends. If it is true that people pursue other things besides pleasure or happiness as ends-in-themselves, as Mill admits, then surely this is to admit that pleasure or happiness is not the sole good.[31] Mill tried to show that these contradictory claims are compatible by introducing the doctrine of acquired ends-in-themselves. It is a psychological truism that we pursue some ends as a means for attaining others. We want money in order to get pleasure. But, it is not always recognized, Mill suggests, that some ends which we pursue first as a means to some other end become, through the operation of the laws of association, ends-in-themselves. We come to pursue wealth for its own sake, for the sake of the pleasure which has come to be associated with it. In this way pleasure becomes an intrinsic part of all our ends, hence pleasure or happiness is the only end we really pursue:

> It results from the preceding consid-
> erations that there is in reality nothing
> desired except happiness. Whatever is
> desired otherwise than as a means to some
> end beyond itself, and ultimately to
> happiness, is desired as a part of happi-
> ness, and is not desired for itself until
> it has become so.[32]

Pleasure or happiness has been shown to be the only end we pursue for its-own-sake. Since the principle of utility is the only principle which would be acceptable to reasonable people, it has been established as the sole criterion of morality.

Mill's proof of the principle of utility is clearly an inductive argument which appeals to what he considers the well-grounded findings of scientific psychology. He does not treat the claim that pleasure or happiness is the sole good as a definition, or as an analytically true proposition, as Moore claimed. Rather he treats it as a substantial practical principle for which egoistic hedonism, properly understood, is the main evidential support. Mill's defense of utility when thus understood becomes more intelligible from the perspective of his radical empiricism, but not necessarily more convincing, because it depends on Mill's ability to solve the problem of induction. What is the traditional problem of induction? Let's take a standard example, "It's seven p.m. in late October in southern Ontario, so the sun will be setting soon." How do we know that the fact that it is seven p.m. in late October in southern Ontario is a sound reason for concluding that the sun will set? Well, we might answer that it has in the past. But how does this substantiate our claim? It doesn't, at least for certain. Just because all observed men are mortal, it doesn't follow that all future men will be mortal, for some men may turn out to be immortal. It is impossible to make a deductively valid move from "some" to "all." It is the observation that inductions are unsound deductive arguments which gives rise to the problem of induction.

Mill's solution to the problem of induction operates at two levels. First, he suggests that all inductions

presuppose a uniformity of nature, for example, that
every event has a cause.[33] Mill thought that very
general facts of experience, like those expressed in the
law of causality or the laws of association, were so
wide-spread throughout our experience that this was
sufficient to justify their use as the axiomatic foun-
dations of scientific and moral reasoning. Second, once
we realize that in inductions we are looking for a
certain kind of uniformity, then the goal of inductive
logic is to establish a set of inference rules which will
enable us to make sound inductions, just as the rules of
deductive logic enable us to make sound deductions.[34] As
Bradley notes, inductive logic for Mill is a matter of
applying rules to particular cases:

> The business of Inductive Logic is to
> provide rules and models (such as the
> syllogism and its rules for ratio-
> cination) to which if inductive arguments
> conform those arguments are conclusive,
> and not otherwise.[35]

The same procedure would apply in ethics. Once we
have established that pleasure is the sole good then all
we would have to do was to generalize from experience to
establish moral rules to guide our conduct.

It is now widely agreed that Mill's attempt to
justify the axiom of uniformity of nature is inadequate.
As Karl Britton remarks:

> Mill completely fails to show how a knowl-
> edge of a general law of causation could
> be derived from experience; and how if we
> had that knowledge, it could constitute a

major premise by means of which particular generalizations could be justified.[36]

It is also widely agreed that the canons of inductive reasoning developed by Mill are not capable of doing the job he wanted them to do. As Bradley pointed out, all of Mill's methods make use of general premises in the form of hypotheses which select, among an infinite set of antecedents, likely causes. They never move simply from particular to particular as Mill claimed they did. For Bradley, universal propositions are involved in all our thinking.[37] The process of selecting hypotheses for testing is the crucial intellectual operation in science but it cannot be guided by a system of rules. Scientific reasoning is essentially a creative process which cannot be reduced to the mechanical application of rules to particular cases. Mill's inductive defense of the principle of utility fails. However it does so not because he tries to deduce moral conclusions from factual premises, but because he failed to provide an adequate account of inductive reasoning in general and of moral reasoning in particular.

If the naturalistic fallacy is a mistake in deductive logic, then Mill did not commit the fallacy. If however it is also a logical mistake to try to arrive at moral conclusions from non-moral premises by inductive methods of argument, Mill might still have committed the fallacy. Even if he had solved the problem of induction, it may still be wrong to try to move from fact to value by inductive methods. We might think that a descriptive ethical enquiry could establish a criterion which everyone actually uses to determine what is right and wrong. We might then have a universal inference rule from which we could derive particular moral conclusions. Even if it is true that everyone's moral reasoning is actually controlled by the principle of utility does it follow that everyone ought to reason as utilitarians do? Clearly not, for we could always invent a better method. Mill seems to be arguing this way when he suggests that all anyone really pursues as intrinsically valuable goals are pleasurable, if complex, ends. If this is what Mill is doing then he could be committing the naturalistic fallacy in this wider sense. In this sense we can formulate the naturalistic fallacy as follows: no moral conclusion can be derived deductively or inductively from a set of non-moral premises. I turn now to Bradley's arguments to see if he committed the naturalistic fallacy in any sense.

Bradley's defense of the principle of self-realization, like Mill's defense of the principle of utility, is clearly not deductive. In Ethical Studies, he was not trying to deduce moral conclusions from metaphysical premises. He does hold that a metaphysical foundation is required to prove that self-realization is the end for man, and in this he differs from Mill. For Bradley all final proofs are metaphysical. But he also thought his basic moral principle could be defended by an appeal to ordinary moral experience and to the well-established findings of scientific psychology. He says:

> Instead of remarking, then, that we lack space to develop our (metaphysical) views, let us frankly confess, that properly speaking, we have no such views to develop, and therefore we can not prove our thesis. All that we can do is partially to explain it, and try to render it plausible.[38]

Bradley thought that the tentative proof this type of argument provided would be sufficient to overthrow the claims of his opponents and provisionally establish the principle of self-realization. It would achieve this by showing that both common sense, and the well-established findings of scientific psychology, supported self-realization as the first principle of morality. He was also well aware of the logical problems involved in trying to deduce moral conclusions from psychological premises. He recognized that the psychological claim "Men can only desire pleasure" does not imply either, that "pleasure ought to be desired" or that "pleasure alone ought to be desired." He says:

> If pleasure were the only thing that could be desired, it would, hence, not follow straight from this that pleasure is desirable at all, or that, further, it is the sole desirable. These conclusions might follow, but in any case not directly; and the intermediate steps should be set out and discussed. The word 'desirable' naturally lends itself to misuse, and has on this account been of service to some Hedonistic writers. It veils a covert transition from 'is' to 'is to be.'[39]

Bradley's attitude towards deductive reasoning is even more negative than Mill's. He agreed with Mill that real inference always produced new knowledge:

> We have no inference at all, we have simply a frivolous show and pretense, if

thinking something we already know we assert the whole or part of this once more, and then say 'I have reasoned and got to a conclusion.' An inference must be more than a vain repetition, and its result is no echo of senseless iteration. It is not mere observation yet it gives us something new.[40]

He also agrees with Mill that syllogistic reasoning does not produce real inferences because it does not give us any new information. He says "It sins against the third characteristic of inference . . ., for it does not really give us any new information."[41] But Bradley's criticisms of syllogistic reasoning are far more radical than Mill's. For example, he holds that the syllogism does not exhaust all the forms of deductive inference:

. . . the syllogism is a chimaera, for it professes to be the model of reasoning and there are reasonings which cannot by any fair means be conformed to its pattern.[42]

And it is not merely that the theory of the syllogism is inadequate. What is wrong is the whole project of trying to reduce reasoning to the mechanical application of inference rules to particular cases, which the theory of the syllogism presupposes:

It is not merely that the syllogism has broken down, and it covers at its best but a portion of the subject. It is that no possible logic can supply us with

schemes of inference. You may have
classes and kinds and examples of reasoning, but you cannot have a set of exhaus-
tive types.[43]

Given Bradley's negative view of formal logic it
would be reasonable to assume that his defense of the
principle of self-realization would not involve deducing
the principle from psychological or metaphysical premises. Nor would it be an inductive defense. For
Bradley, inductive logic was also an inadequate account
of scientific and moral reasoning:

. . . starting from particular perceptions of sense, there is no way of going
to universal truths by a process of
demonstration perfectly exact, and in all
its steps theoretically accurate.[44]

Mill's inductive logic represented another attempt
to reduce reasoning to the mechanical application of
rules to particular cases. But this can't be done
because it fails, like formal logic does, to capture the
creative contextual aspect of thought. For Bradley both
the deductive and inductive models of reasoning are
mistaken:

From the alternative--either an explicit
syllogism or an inference from particulars to particulars--you can hardly fail
to get a false result. You may infer--
the syllogism in extension is no argument, and therefore we go from particulars, to particulars. You may infer--It

is not possible to argue from particulars, and therefore we reason always in syllogisms, explicit and (if you like) also extensional. But to me it is nothing which conclusion you adopt. For both are errors and both at bottom are one and the same error. They are twin branches from one root of inveterate prejudice and false assumption.[45]

The false assumption is the hypothesis that reasoning is a mechanical process. For Bradley inference and reasoning are organic processes, in which data is reorganized into coherent wholes: "The process is an operation of synthesis, it takes its data and by ideal construction combines them into a whole."[46] The process possesses elements of both deductive and inductive reasoning. The theory of the syllogism was right in recognizing that all sound arguments contain at least one universal proposition. The theory of induction was right in recognizing that sense perception is our window on the world. But they were both wrong in the way they conceived the relation between the formal and material aspects of thought. For Bradley all thinking involves ideal experiments in which hypothetical judgements are tested for their ability to organize data into meaningful wholes. Thought is essentially holistic and creative. It involves looking at the data from different hypothetical perspectives, yet it always has a reference to the real world:

A supposal is in short, an ideal experiment. It is the application of a content to the real, with a view to see what the

consequence is, and with a tacit reserva-
tion that no actual judgement has taken
place. The supposed is treated as if it
were real, in order to see how the real
behaves when qualified thus in a certain
manner.[47]

It is like saying, "Imagine it to be like this and
you'll _see_ how everything will fit to-gether." All
thought is hypothetical, tentative and experimental,
hence it cannot produce any absolutely certain conclusions. It is because thought is organic and creative
that we cannot provide a set of rules, or models of
reasoning, which when applied mechanically will produce
certain truth:

The idea of a complete body of models of
reasonings, to be followed as patterns
and faithfully reproduced to make and
guarantee the individual inference, I set
down as a superstition.[48]

Logic, for Bradley, is a descriptive or explanatory
science rather than a prescriptive art, as it was for
Mill and the formal logicians:

Logic has to lay down a general theory of
reasoning, which is true in general and
in the abstract. But when it goes beyond
that, it ceases to be a science, it
ceases to be logic . . ."[49]

The main purpose of logic is to understand the
nature of reasoning, rather than to teach people how to

think critically. Bradley was uncertain about the relevance of logic to practise. He thought it could have a negative function. It might prevent us from approaching practical logic in the wrong way. For example, it could stop us from embarking on the sterile projects embodied in systems of formal logic and Mill's logic of induction:

> By finding the functions made use of in our proofs, we can classify them with a view to further understanding. And we may thus avoid some mistakes in the actual work of reasoning.[50]

He doubted, however, whether the science of logic could have a positive function in practise. He did not think that it would help us to become more logical or to improve our critical thinking:

> In my actual reasonings I myself certainly have never troubled myself about any logic; but I do not know the conclusion which should follow from this, or whether (whatever it may be) it would apply universally. Still, any usefulness in practise falls, I must insist, outside the main end and purpose of a true logic.[51]

Generally Bradley was skeptical of practical logic, even if he didn't close the door on it completely. Given Bradley's understanding of the nature of reasoning, it should be clear that he would not try to deduce moral conclusions from either psychological or metaphysical premises. So he is not committing the naturalistic fallacy in that sense. Nor would he be likely to commit it in any other sense, because he is not trying to provide an inductive defense of the principle of self-realization, as Mill had tried to do for the principle of utility.

This holds, even if we reject Bradley's criticisms of formal and practical logic. These criticisms presuppose that cognitive psychology, which studies the way we actually think, is relevant for prescriptive logics, which deal with how we ought to think. But this presupposition is as controversial as the claim that we can derive moral conclusions from non-moral premises. Can we deduce conclusions about how we ought to think from knowldege of how we actually think? Isn't trying to do so to make a logical mistake similar to the naturalistic fallacy? The answer to the first question is no; the answer to the second question is yes. It is certain that a descriptive logic must have some relation to natural thought processes, if it is to be taken seriously, although the exact nature of the relation may remain problematic. But it is not certain that a prescriptive logic need have any relation to our natural thought processes to be considered true. Cognitive psychology and formal logic may be logically independent of each other. Formal logicians have never thought that their logics mirrored actual patterns of thought. For them formal languages are not the same as natural languages. Formal logics are attempts to improve on the informal thought processes we use in ordinary life. Still the common-sense hypothesis that a prescriptive logic should take into account descriptive logic if it is to succeed in making us more logical is difficult to reject entirely.

In any case, Bradley would not try to deduce pre-scriptions about how we ought to think, from propositions about how we do think, any more than he would try to deduce how we ought to act from how we do act. Nor would he try to move inductively from how we reason to how we ought to reason. Hence Bradley's arguments are not open to the same criticisms Moore used against Mill. Bradley was not interested in improving our logic. In fact Bradley was as suspicious of the value of practical ethics as he was of practical logic, even though he did not close the door on it either. Unlike Mill, Bradley did not see ethics as a practical discipline. For him ethics was a speculative science which constructed theories to explain a specific subject matter, which he referred to as the "moral world." He says:

> All philosophy had to do is to understand
> what is and moral philosophy has to
> understand morals which exist, not to
> make them, or to give directions for
> making them.[52]

The ethical theorist should be distinguished from the moralist. A moralist is someone who sets out not only to defend a system of morals but to proselytize for it. The moralist is a preacher or social reformer. The ethical theorist, on the other hand, is not required to make substantive moral judgements. His job is to under-stand morality, not to make it. He should not try to achieve with theory what can only be achieved through practise. Morality is discovered in the world. It is not created by the theorist. "Ethics has not to make the world moral but to reduce to theory the morality current in the world."[53] The purpose of ethical theory is the development of intellectual, not moral, virtue. Studying ethics is not likely to make you a better person, any more than studying logic will make you more logical. Bradley conceived the task of ethics as constructing theories which would account for the facts of the moral life:

> The fact is the moral world; both on its external side of family, society and state, and the world of the individual in them, and again on its internal side of moral feeling and belief.[54]

The basic data of ethics is the world of the ordinary moral being, all of us when we are not doing theoretical ethics. The world of the thinking, feeling, moral agent living his/her life out in the concrete worlds of family, society and state. Still Bradley does hold that all ethical theory will depend in part on the soundness of the psychology to which it is related. So, he does leave himself with the problem of distinguishing ethics from psychology, which also claims to study man in a morally neutral way. Mill could distinguish between ethics and psychology, because he thought ethics was a prescriptive art while psychology was a science. This path was not open to Bradley, because of the sharp distinction he drew between theoretical and practical ethics. Bradley's answer to the problem of distinguishing ethics from psychology is both complex and interesting. To understand it we need to look at the way he distinguished metaphysics from the special sciences like psychology, logic, physics, and ethics. Bradley rejected the suggestion that the difference between them can be marked by the subject matter they study. For

example, that science is concerned with reality and
metaphysics with value. Science, Bradley argues, is
morally neutral, as Kant had discovered. In order to do
science we need to suspend moral judgements and deal only
with the facts. But metaphysics too is concerned with
reality. So metaphysics must also be theoretical rather
than practical. The difference between metaphysics and
the special sciences is, Bradley suggests, one of purpose
and extent, and not one of different subject matter:

> A limited science is not in principle
> made what it is by having a compartment
> to itself, but by studying what it
> studies with a limited end or in a limit-
> ed way.[55]

Psychology, for example, ". . . abstracts one side
of the living whole and considers that apart."[56] On
Bradley's view the scientific psychologist approaches the
development of the individual mind in a limited way and
for a limited purpose. The scientist is not trying to
understand the development of the individual mind in any
ultimate or final way. He wants only to acquire sufficient knowledge to enable him to solve a particular
problem. Bradley argued that it was possible to study
any phenomena from scientific perspectives which did not
depend on the ultimate truth of their ontological assumptions:

> In the other sciences we know how it is
> done. The so-called principles which
> explain the facts are working hypotheses,
> which are true because they work, and so
> far as they work but which need not be

considered as a categorical account of the nature of things. The Physicist, for example, is not obliged to believe that atoms of ether do really exist in a shape which exactly corresponds to his ideas. If these ideas give a rational unity to the knowledge which exists and lead to fresh discoveries, the most exacting demand upon the most exact of sciences is fully satisfied. The ideas are verified, and the ideas are true, for they hold good of the facts to which they are applied.[57]

Science can proceed without metaphysical truth because it has a limited purpose. In fact the metaphysician has no right to criticize the scientist or to pass off his metaphysical theories as scientifically sound. To do that they would have to compete with rival scientific theories in the appropriate area of specialization. Similarly, metaphysicians who seek some ultimate understanding of the universe can proceed perfectly well without the direct help of the scientist or any other specialist. The scientist has no more right to interfere with metaphysics than the metaphysician has to interfere with science:

As a working point of view, directed and confined to the ascertainment of some special branch of truth, Phenomenalism is of course useful and is indeed quite necessary. And the metaphysician who attacks it when following its own business, is likely to fare badly. But when

> Phenomenalism loses its head and becoming blatant, steps forward as a theory of first principles, then it is really not respectable. The best that can be said of its pretensions is that they are ridiculous.[58]

The inappropriate intrusion of metaphysics into science, or science into metaphysics will produce only bad science or bad metaphysics. Both intrusions are tempting, and both need to be guarded against, if we are to avoid bad science and bad metaphysics. Both the scientist and the metaphysician must know their place. To recognize the distinction between metaphysics and science is a prerequisite for doing either good metaphysics or good science, so in this limited sense, metaphysics which deals with the distinction is primitive. The same situation holds in psychology. Justification in scientific psychology, as in the natural sciences, is purely pragmatic:

> It is the same with psychology. There is no reason why in this science we should not use doctrines which, if you take them as actual statements of fact, are quite preposterous. For the psychologist, as such, is not interested in knowing if his principles are true when taken categorically. If they are useful ways of explaining phenomena, if they bring unity into the subject and enable us to deal with the fresh facts which arise, that is all that, as psychologists, we can be concerned with. Our principles are

> nothing but working hypotheses: we do
> not know and we do not care if they turn
> out fictions when examined critically.[59]

It is true that to proceed scientific psychology must, like all sciences, make some ontological assumptions. It might, for example, have to assume that each person is a unity and that each possesses a personality which endures through time or that mental events cannot be reduced to bodily events. But whether any of these ontological assumptions about the nature of the self are true in any ultimate sense is irrelevant to the science. What holds for psychology holds also for logic:

> You cannot assert that, if a science goes
> right, that science is unable to start
> from false premises. Have not brilliant
> results in the study of nature been
> obtained by the help of working hypothe-
> ses as hardly pretended to be more than
> fictions. And why should not logic if it
> shares the success, share also in the
> falsehood.[60]

This is possible because thought is an organic process. It is at the completion of the process, not the start of it, where truth lies: "It is not the beginning but the end of our reflection which is valid of the real."[61] Of course the special sciences like psychology, logic, and physics, will possess a certain portion of the truth. Metaphysics, however, is more ambitious because its goal is to possess the whole truth:

> We may agree, perhaps, to understand by
> metaphysics an attempt to know reality as
> against mere appearance, or the study of
> first principles or ultimate truths, or
> again the effort to comprehend the uni-
> verse, not simply piecemeal or by frag-
> ments, but somehow as a whole.[62]

Metaphysics is concerned with absolute truth. Nevertheless the justification of a metaphysical theory is, like
scientific theories, essentially pragmatic:

> All theory is an experiment on given
> reality. It is thus also, if you please,
> a hypothesis which is verified in
> practise. A truth is held as true only
> because on trial it comes as an express-
> ion of reality. As that expression which
> we discover to be the only one which
> works or to be at least the one which
> works best.[63]

Bradley's pragmatism differs radically from other
versions of the theory, especially those developed by the
American philosophers, William James and John Dewey.[64]
For Bradley a theory, or hypothesis, can have intellectual as well as practical consequences. A theory can
work well both theoretically or practically. When he
says ". . . there is in the end no truth save working
ideas,"[65] he does not mean that theories have only
instrumental value, or that reason is the slave of
passion, or that thought is essentially prescriptive, or
that the criterion of truth is the practical results of a

theory. For Bradley the criterion of truth is the idea of coherence within an organic system of thought:

> Our actual criterion is the body of our knowledge, made both as wide and coherent as is possible, and so expressing more and more the genuine nature of reality. And the measure of the truth and importance of any one judgement or conclusion lies in its contribution to and its place in our intelligible system.[66]

A theory is justified, if taken as true, it accounts for the relevant data in a most consistent and complete way. The soundest psychological, logical, and ethical theories will be those which account for the development of the individual psyche, the processes of reasoning, and our moral experience, in the most comprehensive and coherent fashion. And they will be further justified if they can be shown to be consistent with each other, that they can be formed into a single organic body of knowledge. Just as ideas must be related to other ideas in an organic rather than a mechanical way, so must systems of ideas. Although the special sciences are distinct from each other, they can still mutually support each other.[67] Logic is interested in the process of reasoning and so too is psychology but their interest is different. For example, in psychology 'ideas' are mental events which occur in a particular psyche, but in logic 'ideas' are taken as symbols which have a meaning beyond their individual instantiations.[68] For psychology an idea is one thing, for logic another. Yet if we try to explain the development of the psyche in mechanical terms we will never be able to arrive at the highest levels of

cognitive activity.[69]   Similarly with ethics.   Ethics is
concerned with the activities of moral agents and so too
is psychology but again their interest is different.   For
ethics moral agents are autonomous persons, for psychology they are something which develops from earlier stages
in which freedom was absent.   Yet as we shall see, if we
try to explain the development of a moral agent along
mechanical lines, we will never be able to explain the
highest levels of moral development.   Although distinct
from each other, ethics and psychology can mutually
support each other as parts of a larger system of knowledge.

In his ethics Bradley is presenting a theory which
he thinks will account for the facts of our moral experience better than any opposing theory.   When he says: "We
make speak of the good, generally as what satisfies
desire,"[70] he is presenting a hypothesis which needs to
be tested by appeal to our moral experience and related
to theories in psychology and logic.   He is certainly not
trying to provide either a deductive or inductive defense
of the principle of self-realization, hence he does not
commit the naturalistic fallacy in either of its forms.

Chapter I: Ethics and Psychology

1   G. E. Moore, Principia Ethica (Cambridge, 1903),
     p. 110.

2   G. E. Moore, Ibid., p. 114.

3   F. H. Bradley, Ethical Studies (Oxford, 1876, Second
     Edition, 1927), p. 65.

4   Aristotle, "Ethica Nicomachea," Translated by
     W. D. Ross, The Works of Aristotle (Volume IX,
     Oxford University Press, 1915), Book X, 1172b. Cf.
     R. M. Hare, "Ethics," Essays on the Moral Concepts
     (MacMillan, 1972), p. 41.

5   J. S. Mill, "Utilitarianism," Collected Works,
     Volume X (University of Toronto Press, 1969),
     p. 234.

6   G. E. Moore, Principia Ethica, pp. 66-67.

7   C. E. Moore, Ibid., p. 67.

8   G. E. Moore, Ibid., p. 12.

9   A. C. MacIntyre, "Hume on 'is' and 'ought,'" Philo-
     sophical Review LXVIII (1959), pp. 451-46. Useful
     discussions of MacIntyre's paper can be found in The
     is/ought Question, edited by W. D. Hudson
     (MacMillan, 1969), pp. 35-82.

10   Cf. R. M. Hare, The Language of Morals, pp. 29-31,
     and pp. 44-45; also "Ethics," in Essays on the Moral
     Concepts, pp. 45-47; also Freedom and Reason, p. 2.

11   Cf. E. W. Hall, "The Proof of Utility in Bentham and
     Mill," Ethics LX, 1940, pp. 1-18.

12   J. S. Mill, "Utilitarianism," Collected Works,
     Volume X, p. 234; C. F. Mill's remarks in Volume X,
     Chapter 1, p. 207, ". . . contribute something

towards the understanding and appreciation of
Utilitarian or Happiness theory and toward such
proof as it is susceptible of."

13 J. S. Mill, A System of Logic, Collected Works,
    Volume VII, Book 11, Chapter III, pp. 183-208.

14 J. S. Mill, A System of Logic, Book III, Chapter 2,
    pp. 294-305, Chapter 10, pp. 446-453, Chapter 11,
    pp. 454-463, Chapter 13, pp. 481-483, Book VI,
    Chapters 7-9, pp. 879-910.

15. R. E. Butts, William Whewell's Theory of Scientific
    Method (University of Pittsburgh Press, Pittsburg,
    1968), "Mr. Mill's Logic," pp. 265-311.

16 J. S. Mill, A System of Logic, p. 302.

17 Cf. S. Lively and J. Rees, Utilitarian Logic and
    Politics (Oxford, 1978), pp. 51-52.

18 J. S. Mill, A System of Logic, pp. 158-162; cf. Karl
    Britton, John Stuart Mill (Penguin, London, 1953),
    pp. 111-139.

19 J. S. Mill, Ibid., p. 160.

20 J. S. Mill, Ibid., p. 183.

21 J. S. Mill, Ibid., p. 183.

22 J. S. Mill, Ibid., p. 193.

23 J. S. Mill, Ibid., p. 195.

24 J. S. Mill, Ibid,, p. 208.

25 J. S. Mill, Autobiography (University of Toronto
    Press, 1981), p. 233.

26 J. S. Mill, A System of Logic, Book VI, Chapter 12,
    p. 943.

27 J. S. Mill, Ibid., p. 949.

28 J. S. Mill, Ibid., p. 949. Cf. "Utilitarianism,"
    pp. 207-208.

29 J. S. Mill, "Utilitarianism," p. 234.

30 J. S. Mill, Ibid., pp. 234-239.

31 J. S. Mill, Ibid., p. 235.

32 J. S. Mill, Ibid., p. 237.

33 J. S. Mill, A System of Logic, pp. 306-314.

34 J. S. Mill, Ibid., pp. 283-287. Cf. Karl Britton, John Stuart Mill, pp. 157-158.

35 F. H. Bradley, The Principles of Logic (Oxford, Second edition, 1922), p. 355.

36 Karl Britton, John Stuart Mill, p. 168.

37 F. H. Bradley, The Principles of Logic, Volume I, pp. 355-369. Cf. Karl Britton, John Stuart Mill, pp. 156-185.

38 F. H. Bradley, Ethical Studies, p. 65 (word in brackets is mine).

39 F. H. Bradley, Appearance and Reality, p. 362, footnote (word in brackets is mine); cf. p. 361, "For the desirable means that which is to be, or ought to be, desired."

40 F. H. Bradley, The Principles of Logic, p. 246, cf. A. Manser, Bradley's Logic (Blackwell, 1983), p. 34.

41 F. H. Bradley, Ibid., p. 248.

42 F. H. Bradley, Ibid., p. 248.

43 F. H. Bradley, Ibid., p. 521; cf. p. 268. Whether Bradley's criticisms of the syllogism would hold against modern symbolic logic is a moot question. But it is interesting that Manser has pointed out that modern logics like the traditional syllogistic logic are mechanical rather than organic systems: "Bradley's objection to such truth-functionality is that it depends on external relations, whereas in actual thinking we deal with internal ones" (Bradley's Logic, p. 161).

44 F. H. Bradley, Ibid., p. 355.

45 F. H. Bradley, Ibid., p. 352-353.

46   F. H. Bradley, Ibid., p. 256; cf. Guy Stock, "Bradley's Theory of Judgement," The Philosophy of F. H. Bradley (Oxford, 1984), pp. 131ff., for a sound account of Bradley's theory of judgement, and compare with A. Manser, Bradley's Logic, pp. 99-118.

47   F. H. Bradley, p. 86; cf. p. 44. Bradley thought that all categorical judgements could be translated into hypothetical judgements, and that hypothetical thinking was more sophisticated than the concrete thinking expressed in categorical judgements; cf. Lionel Rubinoff, F. H. Bradley (Dent & Son, Toronto, 1968), who argues correctly that Bradley has a strong empirical element in his idealism.

48   F. H. Bradley, Ibid., p. 619.

49   F. H. Bradley, The Principles of Logic, p. 269; cf. p. 620.

50   F. H. Bradley, Ibid., p. 529.

51   F. H. Bradley, Ibid., p. 621.

52   F. H. Bradley, Ethical Studies, p. 193.

53   F. H. Bradley, Ibid., p. 193.

54   F. H. Bradley, Ibid., p. 89.

55   F. H. Bradley, "A Defense of Phenomenalism in Psychology," Collected Essays (Oxford, 1969), p. 372, and p. 365.

56   F. H. Bradley, Ibid., p. 371.

57   F. H. Bradley, The Principles of Logic, p. 340.

58   F. H. Bradley, Appearance and Reality, p. 109.

59   F. H. Bradley, The Principles of Logic, pp. 340-341. Cf., Collected Essays, p. 375.

60   F. H. Bradley, The Principles of Logic, p. 589.

61   F. H. Bradley, Ibid., p. 102.

62   F. H. Bradley, Appearance and Reality, p. 1.

63   F. H. Bradley, The Principles of Logic, p. 727.

64   F. H. Bradley, <u>Essays on Truth and Reality</u> (Oxford,
      1914), Chapter 4. "On Truth and Practice,"
      pp. 65-106, Chapter 5, Appendices 1, 2, 3,
      pp. 127-158; <u>Principles of Logic</u>, Volume II, "On
      Theoretical and Practical Activity," pp. 713-728.
      In each of these places Bradley tried to distinguish
      his conception of pragmatism from those of other
      philosophers.

65   F. H. Bradley, <u>Truth and Reality</u>, p. 132.

66   F. H. Bradley, <u>The Principles of Logic</u>, p. 620;
      Manser (<u>Bradley's Logic</u>, p. 106) points out that it
      is the second edition of <u>The Principles of Logic</u>
      (1922) which develops the coherence theory of truth
      with respect to logic and not the first edition
      (1883). The second edition, however, provides a
      richer philosophical basis for defending Bradley's
      ethics than the first edition does, although this
      might not be the case for his logic, as Manser
      suggests.

67   F. H. Bradley, <u>Truth and Reality</u>, p. 69, "An idea is
      true theoretically because and so far as it takes
      place in and contributes to, the organism of knowl-
      edge. And, on the other hand, an idea is false of
      which the opposite holds good."

68   F. H. Bradley, Ibid., pp. 1-10.

69   F. H. Bradley, Ibid., pp. 14-16.

70   F. H. Bradley, <u>Appearance and Reality</u>, p. 356.

CHAPTER II
Utilitarian Moral Psychology

For Bradley ethics and psychology are related because any theory of ethics will presuppose a well-developed view of human nature. Everyone agrees that morality is concerned with good and bad conduct. But conduct involves the realization of purposes, and so is in part a process of self-development. It is through conduct that personality is formed. Morality, for Bradley, is a process of self-realization. The intimate relation between morality and personality formation can be demonstrated through Bradley's critique of moral skepticism, the view that moral knowledge is impossible.[1] The skeptic believes that there is no objective method for establishing the truth or falsity of moral claims, or, at least, that there is no sound reason why anyone should care about being moral. Bradley thinks the skeptical question "Why should I be moral?" is odd. It seems legitimate, but once we ask it, we appear to have left the moral point of view. It is equivalent to asking, "What good is virtue?" A question which presupposes that virtue is good only as a means to something else we want, rather than good-in-itself. So the skeptic implies either (1) everything is good only instrumentally or (2) something else besides virtue is intrinsically good. If he means (1) then he is talking nonsense, because anything which is good instrumentally must be a means to something else which is considered intrinsically good. If (2) he must grant that there is a goal other than virtue, which is intrinsically good. The utilitarians, for example, think this goal is pleasure or happiness, hence virtue for them has only instrumental value. The skeptical question will only make sense if we assume that there is some end which is intrinsically valuable. The question then becomes "what is that end?":

> Has the question, why should I be moral?, no sense then, and is no positive answer possible? No, the question has no sense at all; it is simply unmeaning, unless it is equivalent to, Is morality an end in itself; and if so, how and in what way is it an end.[2]

Even if the skeptic is asserting that being virtuous is not an end-in-itself, this still implies that he understands enough about virtue to know that it is only good as a means. This in turn implies that he knows that something other than virtue is intrinsically good. For Bradley, all negative judgements presuppose a positive ground: "Nothing in the world can ever be derived except on the strength of positive knowledge."[3] The theory of negative judgements is the basis for Bradley's rejection of both metaphysical and moral skepticism. Metaphysical skepticism, which denies the possibility of metaphysical knowledge, is dismissed by Bradley because it is self-contradictory. Metaphysical skepticism rests on a metaphysical assumption: "To say that reality is such that our knowledge cannot reach it is to claim to know reality; . . ."[4] Moral skepticism, like metaphysical skepticism, is self-contradictory. It too presupposes a claim to know something about reality, specifically moral reality. Just as the metaphysical skeptic is a brother metaphysician, so the moral skeptic is a brother moralist. Bradley's criticism of metaphysical skepticism has been strongly attacked by modern philosophers. A. J. Ayer, for example, has argued that the refutation of metaphysics can be reformulated in a way which escapes Bradley's critique.[5] Ayer's anti-metaphysical argument runs as follows. All meaningful propositions are either empirical (true by appeal to sense experience) or analytic (true by definition). Metaphysical propositions are neither empirical nor analytic. Therefore they are pseudo-propositions, which are literally meaningless. Ayer's argument is clearly unsound, as Garrett Vander Veer has shown.[6] Ayer's refutation contains at least one, and possibly two, metaphysical assumptions. First, it leaves unstated the metaphysical status of the verification theory of meaning expressed in the first premise. Second, it assumes that what can exist is equivalent to what can be expressed in our verifiable assertions. In fact the refutation presupposes an empirical metaphysics not vastly different from J. S. Mill's. It is of course no longer fashionable to discuss logical positivism and contemporary philosophers agree correctly that analytic philosophy has developed far beyond the logical empiricism which first gave expression to linguistic analysis. Still the spirit remains in the air, so it is important to remind ourselves that Ayer's argument has never been replaced by a more satisfactory one. And until one appears Bradley's critiques of metaphysical and moral skepticism remain sound.

The moral skeptic's claim that virtue has only instrumental value is suspect, according to Bradley, because it does not square with ordinary moral experience. To ask the question, "Why should I be moral?" is to ask for a justification of morality, but morality is thought to be self-justifying. Ordinarily we believe that morality is the practise of doing good things for their own sake, and not for the external rewards they may bring or the disasters they may avoid. For ordinary morality the rightness or wrongness of an action is determined by appeal to an accepted moral rule, rather than to the actual consequences of the action:

> (The moral) consciousness, when unwarped by selfishness and not blinded by sophistry, is convinced that to ask for the Why? is simple immorality; to do good for its own sake is virtue, to do it for some ulterior end or object, not itself good, is never virtue.[7]

The argument by appeal to our ordinary conception of morality has many similarities to the ordinary language arguments developed by modern philosophers like Moore, Wittgenstein and Austin.[8] Stephen Toulmin in Reason in Ethics developed viewpoints similar to Bradley but couched in linguistic terms. Toulmin maintained that the attempt to justify morality was a mistake that arose from a misunderstanding of the criteria of moral justification which are embedded in our language.[9] Bradley's arguments often take this linguistic form. However for him, unlike Toulmin, there was always an important limitation in any appeal to ordinary language. Bradley recognized that our common assumptions about the nature of things might ultimately be mistaken. So it is always open to us to doubt the deliverances of the common consciousness. Even if we ordinarily believe morality is self-justifying, it doesn't follow that the opposing view is false. Bradley could agree with Ayer's observation that to question a belief which has become entrenched in a language without self-contradiction is always a difficult task. The language already presupposes the falsity of the thesis we wish to defend.[10] Nevertheless it is not illogical to question the ultimate truth of the conceptual systems which control our language. For Ayer the criticism would involve an appeal to empirical science; for Bradley the final appeal would be to metaphysics.

Moral skepticism then, is incoherent. To deny morality is to assert it. To deny that something has value implies that you have a standard for assessing the value of things. The skeptic is someone who is trying to escape from the moral world. He wants to be an amoralist, and ignore the moral aspect of life. But this is existentially impossible. When we choose anything we are making a choice not only about our conduct but about ourselves, about the kind of person we will become. Morality is concerned as much with the creation of good persons, as it is with good conduct. In fact personality formation is the basic goal of morality because we create ourselves through our conduct. It follows that all ethical theories make claims about the ultimate good for man. And these claims are intimately related to the conception of human nature which is explicit or implicit in the theory. For Bradley the good for man is self-realization. He says:

> What remains is to point out the most general expression for the end-in-itself, the ultimate practical 'why'; and that we find in the word <u>self-realization</u>.[11]

The first principle of Bradley's ethical idealism is self-realization or self-perfection, realizing oneself as a harmonious personality! He says: "The end I take to be the fullest and most harmonious development of our being."[12] It is this hypothesis which Bradley defends, first by showing that the best alternative theories, those developed by the Utilitarians and Kantians, do not do justice to the facts of moral experience; second, by demonstrating that ethical idealism, because it is based on a better understanding of human nature, does do justice to our moral experience. If it is to be acceptable an ethical theory it must be able to account for the facts of our common moral world. The theory which does this in the most consistent and complete way will be the theory we should accept as true. Throughout his ethical writings Bradley provided critiques of Utilitarian and Kantian ethics to demonstrate their inadequacy as ethical theories. These critiques are important because they indicate in detail the facts of the moral life any ethical theory is required to explain.

Bradley thought that utilitarian ethics, and the association psychology on which it was based, could not provide an adequate account of our moral experience. In fact, he thought the association theory inadequate for scientific psychology, for logic, and metaphysics, as well as for ethics. He says:

> We have approached a large subject which we can not deal with, and which might well occasion misgiving and doubt. We need give way to neither in our rejection of the principles of the school of association. We reject them in the name alike of metaphysics, of psychology and of logic. [13]

In metaphysics, the theory leads to dogmatic atomism, in logic it provides no adequate account of reasoning, and in psychology it cannot explain the psychological facts which the theory was created to

account for. In ethics it fails to give adequate accounts of moral agency, the role which moral rules play
in our moral experience, the institution of punishment,
and the nature of virtue and vice.

Why does Bradley think that utilitarian psychology
cannot account for moral agency? He begins his argument
with an analysis of our common sense conception of moral
responsibility. For the ordinary person moral responsibility presupposes that man is a moral agent, a free or
autonomous creature who is capable of making up its mind
about right and wrong, of acting on its decisions, and of
taking responsibility for its conduct:

> According to vulgar notions, to be ac-
> countable, a man must act himself, be now
> the same man who acted, have been himself
> at the time of the act, have had enough
> sense to know what he was doing and to
> know good from bad.[14]

To be responsible we must be "free to act" in some
clear sense of that phrase. To be a moral agent is to be
a responsible agent. Morality, as it is commonly understood and experienced, presupposes the idea of freedom.
If morality implies autonomy, then association psychology
will always be inadequate for ethics because it implies
determinism. Association psychology attempts to explain
all human behaviour in terms of efficient causality. It
implies that all human behaviour is determined and hence
can be predicted. Such prediction appears inconsistent
with autonomy and morality. But it is not prediction
itself, Bradley argues, that is incompatible with moral
agency, only prediction of a special kind. What is
acceptable at the common sense level is that behaviour be

predicted on the basis of knowledge of our character or personality: ". . . the prediction which is not objected to, is mere simple prediction founded on knowledge of character."[15] Bradley is correct. We do get upset when people, especially those close to us, fail to predict accurately what we will do on the basis of their understanding of our personality. Don't we frequently say things like "How could you believe I'd do something like that, surely you know me better?" We would be even more distraught, if someone predicted correctly that we would do something evil. But our distress here is not, as Bradley rightly notes, because our action was predicted, but because we cannot now deny a flaw in our character, and one that someone else had detected in us.[16] Predictions based on knowledge of character are acceptable to moral agents: ". . . the man of healthy mind has no objection to the prediction of any actions, which he looks on as issuing from his character."[17] What is not acceptable at the common sense level is what Bradley terms "rational predictions," predictions based on general mechanical laws and some specific data about an individual.[18] These procedures resemble those an astronomer might use to predict the behaviour of a comet. Even "irrational predictions," those based on no grounds at all, would be acceptable to moral agents, because they make no difference to him as a moral agent. If the magician could look into his crystal ball and see our futures, what he will see will be compatible with the development of our characters and not inconsistent with them. What is unacceptable to the moral agent is predictions based on aspects of his experience over which he has no control, which escape the net of his autonomy. We cannot, as moral agents, completely identify ourselves with the irrational elements in our psyches, nor the

behaviour which they issue in. Our basic identity must
be with the organically developing rational whole which
is our character. To try to explain all human behaviour
in terms of mechanical causal laws would be to deny moral
agency and moral responsibility. As Bradley says: "To
explain the origin of a man is utterly to annihilate
him."[19] It annihilates him because it fails to take
account of the fact that we help to make our own characters. Morality is essentially a process of self-creation
which we cannot avoid. So long as we are alive we shall
be acting and in acting, we create ourselves. The most
fundamental question in morality is not what actions are
right and wrong, but what kind of person ought we to be.
Although Bradley believes a person's character is a
product of the interaction between his natural endowment
and his environment, he does not believe that a person's
character can be predicted on the basis of this data, in
accordance with general psychological laws:

> . . . I do not deny that the character of
> a man does follow, as a result, from his
> natural endowment together with his
> environment. . . . But I do say that,
> given the knowledge of a man's innate
> disposition, and given the knowledge of
> his outward world (in the fullest possible
> sense), yet you can not, from these data,
> deduce his character.[20]

A man is after all more than a series of correct
character descriptions and from these alone one cannot
predict his conduct. The kind man may tend to behave in
benevolent ways and it may be useful for practical, or
scientific, purposes to refer to people in terms of this

general description. But this description, nor any set of general descriptions, will not exhaust the character of any one, for each person is a unique individual who is in a process of self-creation.

Mill, of course, like modern utilitarians, believes that association psychology, and the determinism it implies, is consistent with human freedom, and hence with morality. In the System of Logic, Mill argued that it was only a misunderstanding of the doctrine of determinism which led philosophers to assume that it was incompatible with the moral nature of man.[21] Mill's defense of determinism relies heavily on the concept of character, and hence his moral psychology has broad similarities to Bradley's. It will be useful to examine Mill's defense of determinism in some detail to see if Bradley's criticisms of it are valid.

In the System of Logic, Mill saw the issue between libertarians and determinists as one related to the more general question of whether the law of efficient causality applies in the same strict sense to human action as it does to other phenomena. The determinists argue that the law of causality applies to human volitions and actions in the same way as it does to other phenomena. The libertarians argue that the will is not determined like other phenomena by antecedents, but that it determines itself, that is, our volitions and actions are uncaused events.[22] Mill thinks the main reasons why the metaphysical theory of free will was invented was because determinism conflicts with our ordinary experience of volitions and actions, is humiliating to human pride, and is inconsistent with the moral nature of man.[23] Mill admits that determinism is open to these imputations, if it is formulated in the wrong way. But he thinks the doctrine can be formulated in a way which is consistent with the moral nature of man, our ordinary experience of volitions and human dignity.[24] Mill formulates the doctrine as follows:

> Correctly conceived, the doctrine of philosophical necessity is simply this; that given the motives which are presented to an individual's mind and given likewise the character and disposition of the individual, the manner in which you will act might be unerringly inferred; that if we knew the person thoroughly, and knew all the inducements which are acting upon him, we could foretell his conduct with as much certainty as we can predict any physical event.[25]

According to Mill, most people believe that if we knew a person and his circumstances thoroughly, we would not hesitate to predict how he would act. If we have any doubts about doing so, it is because we don't know the other person and his circumstances well enough. Mill believes that human actions are predictable in principle, but not in practise, because the data is either too complex, or to difficult to obtain. It's like predicting the weather. But he does think we can make generalizations from experience which are useful for guiding conduct. Because we could in principle predict human action does not conflict with the ordinary conception of human freedom. In fact, Mill argues, our failure to predict in certain cases is taken as a moral condemnation:

> We do not feel ourselves the less free
> because those to whom we are intimately
> known are well assured how we shall will
> to act in a particular case. We often, on
> the contrary, regard the doubt what our
> conduct will be as a mark of ignorance of
> our character, and sometimes even resent
> it as an imputation.[26]

On this Mill and Bradley could agree. Prediction of human action based on a knowledge of the agent's character is consistent with our ordinary moral experience. Bradley could also agree with Mill's claim that we normally distinguish between a weak and a strong sense of determinism. There are some things we could have done if we had wanted or chosen to, while there are other things we could not have done even if we had wanted to or chosen to. I could, for example, go for a walk around the university grounds, even though I have never done so. But I could not fly around the university grounds by flapping my arms, even if I wanted or chose to. Determinism when applied to human actions means only that a given cause will be followed by an effect unless some other cause counteracts it: "When we say that all human action takes place of necessity we only mean that they will happen if nothing prevents; . . ."[27] We do not feel that we are being forced to do all of the things we do. We feel we could resist most of our desires if we wanted to, and that we could have chosen differently than we did. According to Mill, causal explanations of human action are cases of weak rather than strong determinism.

Our explanations of human actions and natural events both make use of this wider sense of determinism. If X is the cause of Y, and if X happens and Y does not occur, then unless some appropriate explanation, in terms of counteracting causes, can be given why Y did not occur, then X could not be the cause of Y. Similarly, if someone desires X, an action appropriate for acquiring X will follow, and if it does not, then unless some explanation, in terms of counteracting causes, can be given why it did not occur, then X is not really desired. And if someone intends to do X and no appropriate conduct follows, then he does not intend to do X:

> The causes, therefore, on which action depends are never uncontrollable, and any effect is only necessary provided that the causes tending to produce it are not controlled. That whatever happens would not have happened otherwise unless something had taken place which was capable of preventing it, no one surely needs hesitate to admit. But to call this by the name of necessity is to use the term in a sense so different from its primitive and familiar meaning, from that which it bears in the common occasions of life, as to amount almost to a play upon words.[28]

Mill and other utilitarians, like G. E. Moore and Nowell-Smith who followed him, are right in distinguishing between a weak and strong sense of determinism and in suggesting that it is the former sense that captures what we normally mean by freewill.[29] Certainly Bradley would agree. It is not these facts which Bradley is disputing but the way these facts are being interpreted. On the utilitarian view, willing is simply a kind of efficient causality. Mill defines a human action as follows:

> Not one thing, but a series of two things;
> the state of mind called a volition,
> followed by an effect. The volition or
> intention to produce the effect, is one
> thing; the effect produced in consequence
> of the intention, is another thing; the
> two together constitute the action.[30]

Mill is correct in thinking that we normally believe that an intention brings about the action. But he also thinks that this occurs in the manner of one billiard ball striking another and causing it to move. And this is not something we normally believe. In brief, Mill and the utilitarians want to assimilate agent causality to efficient causality, and it is this reduction which Bradley rejects as inconsistent with our ordinary moral experience. And surely Bradley is right. Our ordinary language presupposes a teleological rather than a mechanical analysis of human agency.[31] For us, human action is goal directed. It is thought of as purposeful. Actions are distinguished from events by the fact that agents have intentions or purposes, which bring about conduct. These are teleological explanations, not mechanical ones. We certainly don't mean, for example, that the intention causes the agent to move in the same way that a moving billiard ball is said to cause the one it strikes to move. Of course we do mean that having an intention to do X is followed by doing X unless other forces, internal or external to the agent, intervene. This is similar to what we mean when we say that if X causes Y, then if X happens Y will happen, unless some countervailing forces intervene. Thus we cannot be said to intend to go to the store unless appropriate action, like getting up out of our chairs and going to the closet for our coats, etc., follows. If we continue to sit in our chairs and browse through a book, someone would be entitled to ask us if we really intended to go to the store. Some sort of explanation of why we are not doing anything about going to the store is required. We cannot be said to intend to do X if there is no appropriate explanation available for why we did not do X. What normally needs explanation is not how an agent brings about an action but why, when an agent expresses his intention to do a certain action, the action does not come off. If anyone says he intends to do X and no appropriate conduct follows, then whether he really intended to do X is conjectural, until some appropriate explanation is given.

Our explanations of events share this defeasibility with our explanations of actions, but what counts as an explanation in one case does not always count in the other. If X causes Y, and if X happens and Y doesn't happen, then unless an appropriate explanation can be given why Y didn't happen (someone held his hand on the billiard ball) then X could not be the cause of Y. But we could not say of a billiard ball that it failed to cause the other billiard ball to move because it had decided to do something else, or it had changed its mind about its goals. Teleological explanations are essential to the concept of action. Without notions like intention and purpose we would not be able to understand what an agent was doing. He killed the man. No, he squeezed the trigger on the gun, and the bullet killed the man. Which is the correct description of what happened? We cannot answer without understanding the man's intentions, purposes, etc. When we say that someone did something intentionally or purposefully, we assume that the agent knew what he was doing. The agent is directing his conduct much like a conductor orchestrates his music. It is the general purpose that gives meaning to his conduct. With human action the end and the means are organically, not mechanically, related. Morality is ordinarily defined in terms of that area of experience where the human being can be said to be in control of what is happening. In brief, man must be in the driver's seat for morality, as we understand it, to get going. We do not think that human agency is just something we agree about or make up ourselves. We believe that a human being is a certain kind of being. He/she is a creature who acts in the world, as well as one who responds to the world, a being who is responsible for what he/she does. And this activity cannot be accounted for by either weak or strong determinism which assume that only explanations in terms of efficient causality can count as explanations.

Weak determinism is also unable to account for the distinction we ordinarily draw between will and desire. A decision of the will does not just happen. It must be the effect of some previous cause. It's not just a question of being capable of choosing between alternatives, but of explaining why we chose one alternative rather than another. The weak determinist can only explain will in terms of the strongest desire. If we desire X, we will try to get X, unless we desire something else more than X. The determinist cannot draw a clear distinction between a cause of acting and a reason for acting. Unless some cognitive element is introduced into the analysis, weak determinism will collapse into strong determinism. Mill's answer to this criticism is to suggest that a cognitive element is built into our desires; namely, the perception of the balance of pleasure over pain the desired object will bring:

> . . . those who say that the will follows
> the strongest motive, do not mean the
> motive which is strongest in relation to
> the will, or in other words, that will
> follows what it does follow. They mean
> the motive which is strongest in relation
> to pain and pleasure, since a motive,
> being a desire or aversion, is propor-
> tional to the pleasantness, as conceived
> by us of the thing desired, or painfulness
> of the thing shunned.[32]

Mill is correct to stress that some of our desires possess a cognitive as well as an emotive element. Normally we don't fear anything unless we believe it is dangerous or harmful. But the cognitive aspect which Mill introduces is too restricted to save his theory. Only hedonism has a role to play in the theory. Hedonism itself is not a matter of choice. But this again is inconsistent with our ordinary moral experience, for many people, rightly or wrongly, do not choose hedonism as a way of life.

Another argument against Mill's defense of weak determinism is that it leads to fatalism. A fatalist is someone who believes both that everything we do is determined by past events and that there is nothing we can do to prevent it. The fatalist believes that our conduct follows from our character and that our character is determined by our upbringing. Since our character is made for us, rather than by us, there is no point in trying to alter our characters. However, Mill points our correctly that just as we can do something else if we want or choose, so we can alter our characters, if we choose or want to.[34] If parents have the desire to mould

our characters there is no reason why we can't possess
the desire to re-mould ourselves. Certainly we have no
direct power to re-mould ourselves. But neither do
others have a direct power to mould us. Nor do we have a
direct power to mould others. We cannot simply say to
someone, "be such and such!," and it will necessarily
follow that he/she will be so. We cannot simply will
that our children be what we want them to be. We need to
place them under the influence of certain circumstances
before they become what we should like them to be.
Similarly, we can place ourselves under the right influences, under the poets, for example, and in that way
educate ourselves. Culturalization and self-cultural-
ization operate with the same method: "We are exactly as
capable of making our character, if we will, as others
are of making it for us."[35] If we agree that we can
mould the characters of others, then it would be inconsistent to claim that we cannot re-make ourselves, if we
have the desire to do so. Of course, a fatalist could
argue that this would not settle the matter, for the will
to alter our own character is the result of forces
external to ourselves. It is planted there by someone
else or it is not planted at all. To escape this dilemma, Mill needed to argue that the desire to change
ourselves can be formed by us as well. Mill's method of
doing this is interesting. He says the desire to change
ourselves is formed:

> Not, in general, by our organization, nor
> wholly by our education, but by our
> experience--experience of the painful
> consequences of the character we previous-
> ly had or by some strong feeling of

admiration   or   aspiration   accidently
aroused.[36]

The desire to change our character arises from the
natural disposition of the human being to pursue pleasure
and avoid pain. To be a person of a certain kind is to
suffer mental anguish. To develop into a person of a
certain kind is to suffer mental anguish. If we develop
into a person who suffers mental pain, the desire to
change naturally arises. Fatalism presupposes both the
wish to change ourselves and the feeling that we can't,
and this contradiction is naturally depressing. Fatalism
by itself makes us uneasy, hence its intrinsic instability. Our feeling of moral freedom is, Mill believes,
equivalent to our feeling that we are able to modify our
character if we want to:

> A person feels morally free who feels that
> his habits or temptations are not his
> masters, but he theirs; who even in
> yielding to them knows that he could
> resist; that were he desirous of alto-
> gether throwing them off, there would not
> be required for that purpose a stronger
> desire than he knows himself capable of
> feeling.[37]

Mill is correct, fatalism is intrinsically unstable.
But it is not clear that this instability alone will
generate a change in character. Many people who find it
impossible to cope with their lives remain in this
condition indefinitely. Should we blame them for not
changing themselves? Perhaps their despair was too deep
for them to recover their self-control without help. In

any case, so long as we continue to depend on the law of efficient causality to explain our moral experience, we will be unable to get an adequate understanding of the nature and limits of our freedom. In the end determinism weak or strong removes moral responsibility. If we want to excuse someone from moral responsibility one of the ways to do this is to claim that the person could not help doing what he did. He was in the grip of sociological forces over which he had no control. Bad people are made, like good people, by society. So if any one does something considered to be wrong, society and not the individual should be held responsible. But again this is inconsistent with our normal moral experience. We distinguish between people who can be held responsible for what they do and those who cannot, for psychological or other reasons. In our legal system we have the plea of insanity, yet we do not consider all wrongdoers to be insane.

A final argument of Bradley's against Mill's defense of determinism is that it fails to account adequately for our ordinary idea of punishment. If determinism were true then punishment would be justified only as a means to some other end. It could never be an end-in-itself. Punishment would only be justified if it contributed to the good of society, deterred other potential criminals from committing crimes, or if it benefitted the offender, i.e., reformed him. But this view of punishment is inconsistent with our common-sense view. As Bradley points out, ordinarily we assume that there is a necessary connection between punishment and guilt. Punishment is justifiable only if someone has done something wrong. If punishment is inflicted for any other reason than wrongdoing, then it is unjust:

> Punishment is punishment, only where it is
> deserved. We pay the penalty, because we
> owe it, and for no other reason; and if
> punishment is inflicted for any other
> reason whatever than because it is merited
> by wrong, it is a gross immorality, a
> crying injustice, an abominable crime and
> not what it pretends to be.[38]

It would be immoral to punish someone for our own
convenience, for the good of society, or for the benefit
of the offender. Bradley quotes Kant, approvingly, on
the subject:

> Judicial punishment can never be inflicted
> simply and solely as a means to forward a
> good other than itself, whether that good
> be the benefit of the criminal or of civil
> society; but it must at all times be
> inflicted on him for no other reason than
> because he acted criminally.[39]

Guilt is a necessary condition for punishment. This
substantial moral principle is basic for our institutions
of law and punishment. In order to justify punishment it
first must be clearly established that a law has been
broken. But it doesn't follow that punishment must be
carried out. Guilt for Bradley is a necessary but not a
sufficient condition for punishment. Once the right to
punish is established, all the utilitarian considerations
can enter the picture:

> Having once the right to punish, we may
> modify the punishment according to the

> useful and the pleasant; but these are
> external to the matter, they cannot give
> us a right to punish, and nothing can do
> that but criminal dessert.[40]

For the determinist, however, there is no necessary connection between punishment and guilt. Punishment can only be justified if it protects others or benefits the offender. To punish someone merely for doing something wrong is simply revenge. Revenge, for the utilitarian, is the infliction of useless suffering. What is the point of that? Perhaps no point, but if we take deterrence or reform as the only justifications for punishment, we are led to deny the axiom which is at the core of the institution. The proposition "We ought not punish the guilty" appears self-contradictory because the idea of an act of punishment includes the idea of pain or penalty being inflicted on the person because he/she is guilty of a crime. The act of punishing makes no sense outside the institution of punishment. That is why, as Bradley rightly points out, disciplining a child is not, strictly speaking, a form of punishment. The pain in this case is used to spur the development of the moral agent. Nor is training of a dog a form of punishment. In fact for Bradley it would be wrong to punish a dog for doing something wrong because a dog is not a moral agent:

> We are content to hold the vulgar creed
> that a beast is no moral agent, actual or
> possible; is not responsible nor the
> subject of rights, however much the object
> of duties. According to vulgar notions a
> beast ought not to be punished because he

deserves it, but only to make him better.[41]

To punish an incorrigible person is valid, even if
it does not make him/her better. If determinism were
correct, we would have to equate disciplining children
(who are potential agents) and training dogs (who are not
moral agents) as forms of punishment, which they clearly
are not. These paternalistic activities may be morally
justified but not by appeal to the principles of justice.
In the case of potential moral agents, like children and
adolescents, we might want to talk of diminished responsibility and modify the notion that the innocent not be
punished. Here the principles of justice would be
modified by appeal to the good of potential moral agents
or the good of society.[42] To adopt determinism is to
abandon the moral model of man and substitute for it the
medical model. Punishment becomes medicine for the
criminal and society alike, and individual moral responsibility vanishes. Utilitarianism, and association
psychology, are unable to provide an adequate account of
our institution of punishment. Because it is unable
adequately to account for moral agency determinism is
inconsistent with moral freedom. In spite of the inge-
nious attempts of some modern philosophers and psychologists to prove otherwise, Bradley is correct on this
issue.[43]
The theory does no better when it tries to deal with
the character of moral rules, or the place they occupy in
our lives. For the hedonist moral rules are merely a
means to maximizing pleasure and minimizing pain. There
is no intrinsic value involved in following the rules for
their own sake. As Bradley says:

> You cannot, I object to the Hedonist, make
> these laws part of the end, and identify
> them therewith; for the end was clearly
> laid down as pleasurable feeling and there
> is no essential connection between that
> end and the laws as means. If the laws
> and rules are not feelings (and they are
> not) they must be a mere means to feeling.
> The relation of the two, of the end and
> the means is external.[44]

For the utilitarian moral rules are intellectually
expendable. They are simple generalizations from experience, and hence they have no epistemological force.
Since the rightness or wrongness of a particular action
is determined by its actual consequences, a well-
established particular judgement will always take precedence over a moral rule. Whether the act conforms to the
rule or not is epistemologically irrelevant. As Bradley
says:

> I may be perfectly aware that acting on
> the rules is, speaking generally, the way
> to reach the end. I may even admit that
> the departure from rules in most cases has
> produced, and must produce, an effect
> detrimental to the end. . . . But now the
> matter stands thus: I have taken all
> pains to form an opinion, and I am quite
> certain that my case is an exception. I
> have no doubt whatever that in this
> instance the breaking of the rule will
> increase the surplus. . . . What is this

rule that is to come between me and my
duty.[45]

Since moral rules are merely rules of thumb, or
general policy guidelines, they can always be broken if
an agent sincerely believes that doing so will maximize
pleasure. If punishing the innocent would maximize
pleasure and minimize pain, then it would be just to do
so. The same would be true with adultery:

> The rule says, Do not commit adultery. I
> wish to commit adultery. I am sure I do
> not want to please myself at all, in fact
> the contrary. I am as positive as I can
> be of anything, that the case is either
> not contemplated by the rule, or, if it
> is, that the rule is wrong, that the
> proposed act must diminish the sum of
> pain, and must increase the sum of plea-
> sure of the sentient world as a whole, and
> this too after all consequences I can
> reckon (as I can reckon no more) have been
> counted in. Is it immoral then to break
> the rule; or rather is it not immoral to
> keep it.[46]

The trouble with the utilitarian view of moral rules
is that few, if any, of our moral rules are simple
guide-lines, or inductions from experience. Many moral
rules are the basic building blocks of our social institutions, like law and monogamous marriage. The problem
is not that of exception to rules, because theoretically
any moral rule can have exceptions built into it, but of
the reasons for which exceptions are made, and who is to

authorize exceptions. We may believe it is morally permissible to commit adultery to save the life of a loved one, but not to amuse oneself at the expense of a spouse. In institutional settings it is not up to the individual to decide what reasons are relevant for making exceptions to basic rules, or when they apply. The rules "Punish the guilty" and "No adultery" are not my rules, they are the rules which belong to institutions which I share with others. The point of institutions, like law and monogamous marriage, is to integrate group or interpersonal conduct, in ways which allow the participants to flourish. They are used to harmonize social and interpersonal relations. To be involved in a social practise requires the abdication of one's private judgement and immediate self-interest, to some extent. The question of when my private judgement should take precedence over the moral rules of an institution we are a member of is an important moral question. But it is not automatically true that my private judgement should take precedent in cases of conflict as the hedonistic calculus suggests. In any case the concept of moral rules implicit in utilitarianism does not give an adequate account of the way these rules function in social institutions.

Rule-utilitarianism was developed by modern utilitarians to offset the criticisms of act-utilitarianism. In this new form of the theory, the principle of utility is applied to rules and systems of rules rather than to particular acts. A particular act is right if it conforms to a morally acceptable rule; if it fails to conform, it is wrong. A moral rule or system of rules is shown to be acceptable, if general recognition of the rule or a system of rules promotes the greatest happiness for the greatest number over any alternative rule or system of rules. The rule-theory has many advantages over the act-theory. It enables the utilitarian to distinguish between duty and expediency. It gives moral rules a central role to play in moral thought and allows a complex analysis of the morality of social institutions. It is able, for example, to accept that guilt and punishment are intrinsically related in our system of law, and that principles of justice should take precedence over utility within the system. The system as a whole can then be tested by the principle of utility to determine whether it is a useful social practise.[48]

Although the recent attempts to integrate consequentialist and non-consequentialist values into a single system was an important and fruitful theoretical initiative, rule-utilitarianism could not save utilitarianism. In practise the rule-theory will have to rely ultimately on the act-theory.[49] Since there will always be conflicts of rules, an appeal to the rules themselves cannot resolve moral dilemmas. The final appeal must always be to the direct consequences of each particular action. So in the end the rule-theory is only a more complex application of Mill's position on rules. They are methodologically important but epistemologically irrelevant. Mill himself had toyed with the idea of a rule-theory, and it could be argued that he was developing utilitarianism in that direction. But Mill never questioned the fundamental axiom of the theory that a general rule can always be overridden by a well-established particular judgement.[50]

Utilitarian ethical theory fails to deal satisfactorily with moral agency, the institution punishment and generally with the function of moral rules in social institutions. It is also unable to deal adequately with the self or personality. Association psychology attempts to reduce the self to a mere collection of isolated mental events, held together by the laws of association. As Bradley remarked, rather unkindly, of Alexander Bain, the eminent 19th-century association psychologist: "If Mr. Bain collects the mind is a collection. Has he ever thought who collected him."[51]

A collection of discrete, externally related events, cannot be aware of itself. Self-consciousness, a basic datum of human mental life, remains unexplained. Since personality is central to our moral experience, and utilitarian psychology is unable to account for it, so it again proves itself inadequate as a moral psychology. No matter what we do, we will make something of ourselves. So the question is not whether to create ourselves or not, but rather what kind of self ought we to create. What end shall we choose to pursue? What goal do we think possesses the greatest intrinsic value? Utilitarianism, like all ethical theories, has a theory of virtue and an end to offer us. The end that is offered is pleasure. For the utilitarian a virtue is a disposition which benefits the agent (personal virtue) or which benefits others (moral virtue). A virtue for a utilitarian possesses only instrumental value. It is a means to pleasure or happiness. It does not itself possess intrinsic value. But this, as we saw, is inconsistent with ordinary moral experience.[52] For morality, virtue is the practise of doing good things for their own sake and not for some external reward. Virtue is intrinsically, and not merely instrumentally, valuable. Hedonism as a philosophy of life has always had strong appeal to mankind; yet, as Bradley correctly notes, the one thing most agree on is that pleasure is not a practical end to pursue. It is impractical because by its nature it is not something we can easily pursue as an end-in-itself. In order to get as much pleasure as we

can we have to take up some other form of life, and
pursuing this get what pleasure we can by the way. As
Bradley observes:

> We take a certain quantity of pleasure, and
> absence of pain as a fair amount, which we
> may call happiness, because we feel that
> we can do with it: and to get this amount
> we take up some way of living, which we
> follow, in general without thinking of
> pleasure. If opportunity offers delights
> by the way, we take them, but without
> inconveniencing ourselves, without leaving
> the road too far, and without thinking too
> much about it.[53]

We can pursue honour, wealth, power, knowledge, sex
or virtue, and all these ends can give us pleasure, but
it is not pleasure that we pursue. In order to get
lasting pleasure we must abandon it as a goal possessing
intrinsic value. If we try to pursue pleasure as an
end-in-itself we will create a paradoxical personality.
The pursuit of pleasure, apart from other goals, produces
the voluptuary, the pleasure-seeker who can never be
satisfied:

> Pleasures, we saw, were a perishing
> series. This one comes, and the intense
> self-feeling proclaims satisfaction. It
> is gone and we are not satisfied. It was
> not that one then, but this one now; and
> this one now is gone. It was not that
> one, but another and another; but another
> and another do not give us what we want;

> we are still left eager and confident
> until the flush of feeling dies down, and
> when that is gone there is nothing left.
> We are where we began so far as getting
> happiness goes; and we have not found
> ourselves and we are not satisfied.[54]

There are, according to Bradley, no fully developed voluptuaries. The pure voluptuary is existentially an impossibility. One can only approximate to, but never fully realize, the pure voluptuary:

> There never was anyone who did not desire
> many things for their own sake; there
> never was a typical voluptuary: and yet
> the pursuit of pleasure does to a certain
> extent exist, and a man approaches the
> ideal voluptuary so far as he makes
> abstract pleasantness his object.[55]

The voluptuary is ontologically unstable, hence to be a voluptuary cannot be a viable human goal. Mill certainly would have accepted the initial claim that utilitarian psychology did imply that pleasure was the sole intrinsic good. But he would have rejected the claim that the only intelligible form of hedonism was that of the voluptuary. The view of life which Mill thought hedonism most consistently presented was not unlike that which Bradley ascribed to common sense morality. Mill says:

> The happiness which they meant was not a
> life of rapture, but moments of such in an
> existence made up of few and transitory

pains, many and varied pleasures, with a
decided predominance of the active over
the passive, and having as the foundation
of the whole not to expect more from life
than it is capable of bestowing.[56]

Mill's pleasure-seeker is not a voluptuary. Nor is
he the man of lust who wallows in bestial pleasures.
Mill carefully distinguished between what he called the
higher and the lower pleasures, those which are essentially mental and active, and those which are essentially
bodily and passive. Mill says:

. . . there is no known Epicurean theory
of life which does not assign to the
pleasures of the intellect, of the feelings and imagination, and of the moral
sentiments a much higher value as pleasures than those of mere sensation.[57]

Man shares with animals appetites for food, drink,
sex, and other bodily pleasures or lower pleasures, but
the higher pleasures, the active pursuit of truth,
goodness and beauty, are distinctively human. Without
the higher faculties and their accompanying pleasures, no
human can be fully satisfied. In fact most people with
any range of practical experience tend to choose the
higher, active, rather than the lower, passive, pleasures:

Now it is an unquestionable fact that
those who are equally acquainted with and
equally capable of appreciating and
enjoying both do give a most marked

preference to the manner of existence which employs their higher faculties.[58]

It is not the voluptuary who emerges from Mill's hedonism, but the self-reliant, rational pleasure-seeker. The higher pleasures differ in kind from the animal or bodily pleasures, and hence they have greater value for humans. The higher pleasures are not only instrumentally better than the lower pleasures, they are intrinsically better. Mill says:

> It must be admitted, however, that utilitarian writers in general have placed the superiority of mental over bodily pleasures chiefly in the greater permanency, safety, uncostliness, etc., of the former--that is, in their circumstantial advantages rather than their intrinsic value.[59]

Mill's claim that the mental pleasures are intrinsically better than the bodily pleasures is, one would suspect, a reflection of the middle-class Victorian morality he came to represent. A morality less consistent with the hedonism than Mill thought it was. Bradley argued, correctly, that the distinction between the higher and lower pleasures obscured the real difference we normally draw between pleasure and happiness. If you try to distinguish higher from lower pleasures on non-quantitative grounds then you have abandoned hedonism, you no longer assent to the principle that "pleasure is the sole intrinsic good." Bradley says:

> Higher then . . . has no meaning at all
> unless we go to something outside plea-
> sure, for we may not go to quantity of
> pleasure. But if we go outside pleasure,
> we not only have given up the greatest
> amount of theory, but we have thrown over
> Hedonism altogether.[60]

Qualitative distinctions in pleasure can only be
meaningful if one begins to take pleasure as an aspect of
more complex mental states, like wanting or desiring, in
which the agent's goal is rarely pleasure. One may
pursue virtue, power, or practical wisdom, and these
activities may be inherently enjoyable, but to pursue
these ends is quite different from pursuing pleasure for
the sake of pleasure. As Timothy Sprigge has shown,
idealism and utilitarianism can be synthesized if
utilitarianism substitutes an organic for its mechanical
conception of pleasure or happiness. He rightly points
out that this conceptual shift is required to make sense
of Mill's distinction between higher and lower pleasures.
If this is done a common ground can be established
between the two theories but at considerably more theoretical cost to the utilitarian than the idealist.[61]

Bradley also argues correctly that the hedonist
doesn't need Mill's qualitative pleasures to mark the
difference between the higher and the lower pleasures.
To say that the higher pleasures were intrinsically
better than the lower pleasures would be, if one remained
a consistent hedonist, to say that they produce a greater
amount of pleasure for any individual than the lower
pleasures do. This might not be saying a great deal, but
at least it is consistent with hedonism. As Bradley
says:

Here the principle of the greatest amount
of pleasure is adhered to, that is the
top, and what approaches it or contributes
to it is nearer the top. But since the
moral 'higher' is here, as we see, the
more pleasurable or the means to the more
pleasurable, we come in the end to the
amount, the quantity of pleasure without
distinction of kind or quality; and having
already seen that such an end is not a
moral end, we get nothing from the phrases
'higher' and 'lower' unless it be con-
fusion.[62]

The consistent utilitarianism can never escape the
voluptuary because the theory confuses a natural learning
mechanism, the experience of pleasure and pain, with an
end which is distinct from it, the realization of ends
which control the growth of the self. Pleasure will
always be part of the good, but it cannot be the ultimate
end for man. Bradley recognized that hedonism can also
be transformed into a form of rational selfishness, as
Mill suggested it could. What this produces is not the
pure voluptuary but his near cousin, the calculating
pleasure-seeker who uses everyone as a means to his own
gratification:

. . . he treats all objects as means, that
he cares for none in itself, but will
sacrifice any with readiness, and when you
inquire what is common to them all, you
find that they minister to his personal
comfort.[63]

This cold fish, who is marked by an extreme indifference to the welfare of others, cannot save hedonism. Although the end which the selfish person pursues is concrete rather than abstract, it still stunts the growth of personality, and makes the emergence of a genuine moral agent impossible. The selfish person must always treat others as a means to his/her ends and never as ends-in-themselves. He/she is incapable of impartiality and hence can never respect others as moral agents who possess intrinsic value. If we can never treat others as ends-in-themselves, we can never be moral agents. For Bradley utilitarianism, association psychology, determinism, and hedonism all fall together, and we must look elsewhere for an adequate theory of ethics.

NOTES

Chapter II: Utilitarian Moral Psychology

1   F. H. Bradley, Ethical Studies, pp. 58-64. Cf.
    R. Wollheim, F. H. Bradley (Penguin Books, 1959).
    Wollheim correctly noted the similarity between
    Bradley's argument and H. A. Pritchard's famous
    essay "Does Moral Philosophy Rest on a Mistake?",
    Mind, 1912.
2   F. H. Bradley, Ethical Studies, p. 125.
3   F. H. Bradley, The Principles of Logic, p. 125.
4   F. H. Bradley, Appearance and Reality, p. 1.
5   A. J. Ayer, Language, Truth and Logic (Dover, New
    York, 1952), pp. 33-45.
6   G. L. Vander Veer, Bradley's Metaphysics and The
    Self (Yale, 1970), pp. 1-7.
7   F. H. Bradley, Ethical Studies, p. 62. The brackets
    are mine.
8   Cf. Wittgenstein, Philosophical Investigations
    (Blackwell, Oxford, 1958); J. L. Austin, How To Do
    Things With Words (Oxford, 1962); G. E. Moore,
    Principa Ethica.
9   S. Toulmin, Reason in Ethics (Cambridge, 1958),
    pp. 202-221.
10 A. J. Ayer, "Philosophy and Language," The Concept
    of a Person (MacMillan, London, 1963), pp. 1-35.
11 F. H. Bradley, Ethical Studies, p. 64.
12 F. H. Bradley, Truth and Reality, p. 86.
13 F. H. Bradley, The Principles of Logic, p. 342.
14 F. H. Bradley, Ethical Studies, p. 37.
15 F. H. Bradley, Ibid., p. 9.
16 F. H. Bradley, Ibid., p 16, footnote 1.
17 F. H. Bradley, Ibid., pp. 15-16.

18   F. H. Bradley, Ibid., pp. 16-19.

19   F. H. Bradley, Ethical Studies, p. 18.

20   F. H. Bradley, Ibid., p. 22.

21   J. S. Mill, A System of Logic, Collected Works
       (Volume VIII, Toronto, 1974), pp. 836-843.

22   J. S. Mill, Ibid., p. 836.

23   J. S. Mill, Ibid., p. 836.

24   J. S. Mill, Ibid., p. 836.

25   J. S. Mill, Ibid., pp. 836-837.

26   J. S. Mill, Ibid., p. 837.

27   J. S. Mill, Ibid., p. 839.

28   J. S. Mill, Ibid., p. 839.

29   Cf., G. E. Moore, Ethics (Oxford, 1912), pp. 84-95;
       P. H. Nowell-Smith, Ethics (Penguin Books, 1954),
       pp. 270-314; and J. L. Austin, "Ifs and Cans," for a
       useful critique of these modern versions of Mill's
       arguments.

30   J. S. Mill, A System of Logic, Collected Works
       (Volume VII, Toronto, 1973), p. 55.

31   Cf. G. E. M. Anscombe, Intention (Oxford, 1958); and
       Charles Taylor, The Explanation of Behaviour
       (London, Routledge & Kegan Paul, 1964), pp. 3-71.

32   J. S. Mill, Sir William Hamilton, Collected Works
       (Toronto, 1979), p. 468.

33   J. S. Mill, A System of Logic (Volume VIII), p. 840.

34   J. S. Mill, Autobiography, Collected Works (Toronto,
       1981), p. 177.

35   J. S. Mill, A System of Logic (Volume VIII), p. 840.

36   J. S. Mill, Ibid., pp. 840-841.

37   J. S. Mill, Ibid., p. 841.

38   F. H. Bradley, Ethical Studies, pp. 26-27.

39   F. H. Bradley, Ibid., p. 28, footnote 1.

40   F. H. Bradley, Ibid., p. 27.

41   F. H. Bradley, Ibid., pp. 31-32, footnote 2.

42 F. H. Bradley, "Some Remarks on Punishment," Collected Essays, pp. 149-164.

43 Cf. B. F. Skinner, Beyond Freedom and Dignity (Bantam/Vintage, New York, 1972).

44 F. H. Bradley, Ethical Studies, pp. 105-106.

45 F. H. Bradley, Ibid., p. 107.

46 F. H. Bradley, Ibid., pp. 107-108.

47 Cf. David Lyons, Forms and Limits of Utilitarianism (Oxford, 1965) and my article, "Utilitarianism Old and New," Queen's Quarterly (Volume LXXIV-2, 1967), pp. 330-340.

48 Cf. Rawls, "Two Concepts of Punishment," Philosophical Review (1955), pp. 3-32.

49 Cf. my The Moral Question: Ethical Theory, TV Ontario, 1982, pp. 24-26.

50 J. S. Mill, "Utilitarianism," Collected Works (Volume X), p. 210.

51 F. H. Bradley, Ethical Studies, p. 39. Bradley withdrew his strong criticism of Bain in The Principles of Logic, p. 344, "Though the temptation was irresistible, I am sorry that I treated Bain, here and elsewhere with so little respect."

52 Cf. D. Hume, An Inquiry Concerning the Principles of Morals (1957); J. S. Mill, On Liberty (Bobbs Merrill, 1956), pp. 91-114, and James Mill, Analysis of the Phenomenon of the Human Mind (Second edition, 1869, reprint 1967, New York) (Volume 2), pp. 280-327.

53 F. H. Bradley, Ethical Studies, p. 100.

54 F. H. Bradley, Ibid., p. 96.

55 F. H. Bradley, Ibid., p. 263.

56 J. S. Mill, "Utilitarianism," Collected Works (Volume X), p. 215.

57 J. S. Mill, Ibid., p. 211.

58   J. S. Mill, Ibid., p. 211.

59   J. S. Mill, Ibid., p. 211.

60   F. H. Bradley, <u>Ethical Studies</u>, pp. 119-120.

61   T. L. S. Sprigge, "Utilitarianism and Idealism: A
     Rapprochement," <u>Philosophy</u>, 1985, pp. 447-463.

62   F. H. Bradley, Ibid., pp. 118-119.

63   F. H. Bradley, Ibid., pp. 274-275.

CHAPTER III
Kantian Moral Psychology

If utilitarian psychology could not provide an adequate foundation for ethics, where could Bradley turn to find one? The most promising alternative was a form of rational or metaphysical psychology developed by Kant. Kant, of course, had rejected metaphysical or rational psychology as a viable method for acquiring knowledge of the self.[1] One could not, Kant thought, start with a few simple self-evident truths about the self, e.g., I exist thinking, and deduce, without reference to experience, a true set of psychological propositions, as some rationalists had tried to do. Just as a purely deductive a priori science of nature was inadequate for physics, so a purely deductive a priori science of man was inadequate for psychology. Scientific psychology gave the only reliable knowledge we could have about the self, even though Kant believed that rational psychology must be valid if our moral experience was to be real. Kant, like Bradley, held that utilitarian psychology was inadequate for ethics. But he also held that a form of rational psychology, one presupposing human freedom, was adequate of ethics. It might appear, at first glance, that Kant's psychology could be used as a basis for ethics, because it was founded on the recognition that morality presupposes moral agency. Kant saw that if we were not free to think as we please, and do as we will, then we cannot be held responsible for our conduct. Absence of responsibility implies no morality. He also understood that association psychology could not provide an adequate foundation for morality because it implied determinism, and denied human freedom. Kantianism, like utilitarianism, has an end to offer man.

Rather than pleasure, it recommends that we ought to pursue "The good will":

> The end is will for the sake of will; and, in its relation to me, it is the realization of the good will in myself, or of myself as the good will. In this character I am an end to myself, and I am an absolute and ultimate end. There is nothing which is good, unless it be the good will.[2]

The proper goal for man is moral virtue. To do our duty simply for the sake of duty and not for ulterior rewards, like pleasure or happiness. Moral virtue as a goal for man is acceptable to common sense morality. It is an end which does not fall outside of the self, and so does not treat morality as a mere means to some higher good. It recognizes that the end for man is the creation of a person of a certain kind. So far so good. But not good enough for Bradley. Kant's psychology certainly implies a free moral agent, but not the right kind. It simply substitutes non-determinism for determinism:

> . . . Free will means non-determinism. The will is not determined to act by anything else; and further it is not determined to act by anything at all.[3]

Explanation of human behaviour is dropped completely and every free action becomes a miracle. No prediction is possible on this theory, not even in terms of character or personality. Kantian freedom, according to Bradley, is the freedom of a purely rational creature, one who acts in accordance with purely formal principles, and this implies that to be free, we must be free from all desire. We are not determined by that system of desires and habits we call our character:

> The doctrine of Indeterminism asserts that the actions are in no case the result of a given character, in a given position. The self, or the will, of Indeterminism is not the man, not the character at all, but the mere characterless abstraction, which is <u>free</u> because it is indifferent. It has been well called 'a will which wills nothing.'[4]

Kantian freedom, when properly understood, is an empty formalism. "Duty" turns out to be a merely formal concept which has no empirical (sensous/particular) content: "The standard, we saw, must be formal; it must exclude all possible content because content is diversity. . . ."[5] The theory presents us with a simple goal and with a simple maxim for realizing it: be self-consistent:

> Our practical maxim, then, is, realize non-contradiction. Realize, i.e., act and keep acting; do not contradict yourself, i.e., let all your acts embody and realize the principle of non-contradiction; for so only can you realize the formal will which is the good will. Whatever act embodies a self-contradiction is immoral. Whatever act is self-consistent is legal. Whatever act is self-consistent, and is done for

the sake of realizing self-consistency,
and for the sake of nothing else, is
moral.[6]

Although Bradley does point out that his account of
Kantian Ethics is neither complete nor accurate, he
believes his criticisms of it, criticisms which are
essentially Hegel's, are sound.[7] Kant, according to
Bradley, is a formalist in ethics. Kant's categorical
imperative is a purely formal principle which cannot be
applied in particular contexts. Formalism, any ethics
based on formal logical rules alone, always cuts off
moral thought from lived experience. Lived experience is
unique, sensual, particular; logic is universal, abstract, formal, its exact opposite. How can the latter
ever be a practical guide for the former? This criticism
of Kant is one which Mill would readily endorse. Mill
believed that the will was the child of desire, and, like
Hume, that reason was ultimately the slave of passion.
As Hume says:

> The end of all moral speculation is to
> teach us our duty; and by proper represen-
> tation of the deformity of vice and the
> beauty of virtue to beget corresponding
> habits, and engage us to avoid the one and
> embrace the other. But is this ever to be
> expected from inferences and conclusions
> of the understanding, which themselves
> have no hold on the affections or set in
> motion the active powers of man? They
> discover truths; but where the truths
> which they discover are indifferent and

begat no desire or aversion, they can have no influence on conduct or behaviour. [8]

Unless moral considerations are somehow related to our interests, wants, or desires, they will never provide a motive for acting. Formalism cuts moral thought off from psychological reality, and so emasculates it. If Bradley were right this would be a serious defect in Kant's ethics. But is Bradley right about Kant? The answer would appear to be no, because Kant is not a pure formalist in ethics, anymore than he was a pure formalist in his theory of knowledge. He was no more a formalist in ethics than he was in metaphysics. Kant did not believe that moral rules expressed analytic propositions, propositions which could be shown to be true or false by appeal to the rules of formal logic alone. He thought they were synthetic a priori prescriptions, which needed to establish some meaningful connection with actual experience before they could be justified. In order to show both that Kant is not a formalist in ethics and that formalism in ethics doesn't work, it will be useful to examine in some detail how Kant applies the different forms of the categorical imperative to establish moral prescriptions.

Kant formulates the categorical imperative in both formal and substantive ways. The formal expression of the principle is: "Act only according to that maxim whereby you can at the same time will that it should become a universal law."[9] This is the principle of universalizability: "If we call something a good X, then we are committed to calling anything like it a good X."[10] There are several substantive formulations but we need only consider one here: "Act in such a way that you treat humanity, whether in your own person or in the person of another, always at the same time as an end and never simply as a means."[11] This is the principle of respect for persons: "Always treat persons as ends-in-themselves and never merely as a means."[12] According to Kant, then, an action is morally wrong if it cannot be coherently universalized, or if it sanctions disrespect for persons; if it can be coherently universalized or if it expresses respect for persons, it is morally right. The principle of universalizability is the only formulation that is vulnerable to Bradley's attack, because it is formal. The principle of respect for persons is not vulnerable because it is not a purely formal principle. But even the formal principle is stronger than Bradley believes it to be. Kant never applies the formal principle except in particular contexts. It is the context which supplies the matter for the formal principle. Kant also distinguished between different classes of duties and the principle of universalizability functions differently depending on the type of duty which is under consideration. He classified moral duties into four kinds. The following chart depicts his classification and his examples:

	Duties to the Self	Duties to others
Perfect	No Suicide	Keep Promises
Imperfect	Self-Perfection	Help the Needy

For Kant a perfect duty is one that cannot be overridden by personal preference or inclination but only by a higher duty. An imperfect duty is one that is subject to personal discretion.[13] For example, the obligation to keep a promise can only be overridden, if at all, by a higher duty, like saving a human life. But the obligation to help the needy is less specific. We are morally required to be charitable but to whom, when, and how is left to our discretion.

Kant believed we had a perfect duty to ourselves never to commit suicide. He thought it morally wrong for us to take our lives in order to avoid great suffering. Active euthanasia directed towards the self would always be wrong for Kant. To take our lives from self-interest is always wrong because it is self-contradictory. Kant's formal argument against suicide is not easy to grasp. But if we imagine ourselves as Gods creating the universe in accordance with the law of non-contradiction, we might see what Kant was driving at. In such a universe, according to Kant, a natural instinct towards self-interest could not serve both the preservation and the destruction of life. A rational creator would not produce an inconsistent natural law. When Kant applies the principle of universalizability he always applies it in a context, and here the context is in part supplied by the concept of natural law. Kant says: ". . . the universal imperative of duty may be expressed thus: Act as if the maxim of your action were to become through your will a universal law of nature."[14] A recognition that Kant always applies the principle of universalizability in a context demonstrates that Kant is not a pure formalist in ethics as Bradley claimed he was. But it does not make his formal argument against suicide from self-interest more convincing. In the argument Kant assumes that death can never be in one's self-interest. If someone is suffering from an incurable disease which causes intractable pain, and if there is no hope of escape until death, then surely we can argue that suicide may be in that person's interest.

Kant also held that suicide from self-interest is inconsistent with the principle of respect for persons.[15] Suicide from self-interest displays a lack of respect for one's personal worth. It implies we have low self-esteem. We see our life as worthless. We have no self-respect. But this is to deny that we are moral agents who possess intrinsic value. Our life is intrinsically worthwhile no matter what its quality. This is a more compelling argument because it is primarily substantive rather than formal. The principle of universalizability is still applicable to it, but the argument gets its grip from the content, not the mere form. The argument may not be ultimately valid even on Kantian grounds for we can interpret the capacity to be moral as a specific quality of life. If we do this, it would follow that active euthanasia might be justified when human life had lost this capacity. Nevertheless the substantive argument is stronger than the purely formal one, and it is clearly more fruitful for practical ethics.

Kant believed we have an imperfect duty to perfect ourselves.[16] We ought to perfect our natural talents, but how we do so is up to the individual. If someone is intelligent he/she has a duty to develop this gift of nature, but whether it is developed in science, art, or philosophy is up to the individual. If I were to vegetate and spend all my time on idle enjoyments that might be alright. I would have some sort of existence, if not the most valuable one. But if everyone were slothful then no one would find it easy to be slothful, for sloth depends on the work of others, and a slothful society is always in danger of collapse. Everyone's being slothful is not formally self-contradictory, but it is practically self-defeating, so it still expresses a contradiction in the will. Kant's argument again is plausible because the principle of universalizability is applied in a practical rather than a theoretical context.

The attack on sloth is even stronger, when an appeal is made to the principle of respect for persons. Kant suggests that to vegetate is not to directly degrade oneself but it does not show self-respect either.[17] Sloth leads to spiritual inertia and eventually undermines our capacity for moral agency. The less we do with ourselves, the less we will be capable of doing. In the end we may be able to do nothing at all. Generally the farther removed Kant's arguments are from purely formal ones, the more compelling they become. In significant moral thought the form and content of our lives are simply different aspects of the same experience.

Kant also believed that we have a perfect duty to others not to make promises we don't intend to keep.[18] He thought it was morally wrong to make a false promise in order to get out of trouble. The rule, "everyone ought to make lying promises," is inconsistent. Kant says:

> He then sees at once that such a maxim could never hold as a universal law of nature and be consistent with itself, but must necessarily be self-contradictory.[19]

If everyone was a lying promiser, then no one could be a lying promiser. Kant's formal argument against false promising is again difficult to grasp. It appears to be just a form of utilitarian generalization. If everyone was a lying promiser, then the results would be disastrous, because the socially useful practise of promising would be endangered.[20] This interpretation

misunderstands Kant's argument. His point is similar to
one made by Austin, Rawls and Searle, who argue that
rules like "one ought to keep one's promises" and "Only
the guilty ought to be punished" are constituent of the
practises of promising and punishing.[21] These rules
express values which are intrinsic to the practises. To
deny this is to deny the morality the practises represent. So long as we are participants in a practise, then
we ought to abide by its inherent rules. We ought not to
make false promises or punish the innocent simply because
it's convenient for us to do so. Kant is making an
important observation about the way moral values function
in social institutions. His analysis, it seems to me, is
right, as far as it goes. But Kant treats social practises as if they were natural rather than conventional,
and this is mistaken. If we want to challenge a social
practise this involves challenging its central values.
As R. M. Hare has shown, it is possible consistently to
assent to a rule which denies the inherent value of a
practise if we want to challenge the practise as a
whole.[22] The person who believes that blood sports, like
hunting, are morally wrong does not formally contradict
himself/herself when he/she asserts that one ought not to
use live ammunition when hunting. What is being said is
paradoxical, because of the values inherent in the sport,
but no formal contradiction is involved. The moral rules
which structure social practises are synthetic a priori
prescriptions and are not analytic. They can be sensibly
contradicted, but to do so is tantamount to rejecting the
practise. What is inconsistent is to accept the practise
and not play by the rules which are inherent in it. Once
again Kant's arguments are more plausible when they cease
to be purely formal. Still they are not completely
convincing, because the principle of universalizability

does not provide a criterion for judging the morality of practises like promising and punishing.

Kant also believed that false promising was a violation of the principle of respect for persons.[23] False promising always involves deceiving the promisee. The false promiser is using the promisee as a mere means to his/her ends, because the promisee is being used without his/her consent. A moral agent has a right to informed consent. This is why a surgeon must have the patient's consent before he/she operates. Acting on the principle of respect for persons involves respecting the legitimate rights of others. The principle of respect for persons provides a criterion for assessing the morality of social institutions. The institution of punishment is consistent with respect for persons provided the link between guilt and punishment is retained. Treating criminals as if they were mentally ill, or suffering from a social disease, would not, because this denies that they are moral agents. So is the institution of promising, because it involves the principle of informed consent. Kant's attack on false promising is again stronger when based on respect for persons rather than on universalizability alone. When form and content combine the arguments come to grips with real moral experience.

Kant also believed that we have an imperfect duty to help others in need.[24] We have a duty to be charitable but to whom and how is left to the individual. Kant, like Mill, did not think that other people had a right to our good offices. They have a right to justice but not benevolence. The rule, "Never help others in need," is not formally self-contradictory, but it is practically self-defeating. If everyone refused to help others in need, then no one would help us when we were in need.

But no rational person would assent to the rule, because it requires an impossible kind of self-reliance. R. M. Hare has argued correctly that a fanatic who puts the ideal of self-reliance above immediate self-interest could formally assent to the rule without an inconsistency of will.[25] But the fanatic would be someone who has for the most part lost touch with reality. His rationality would be purely abstract and formal and hence unreal.

Kant also defended benevolence by appeal to the principle of respect for persons.[26] According to Kant, refusing to help others in need is in one sense consistent with respect for persons, but in another sense it isn't. So long as we respect the legitimate rights of others, and do not injure them, we are negatively in accord with respect for persons. We are doing no wrong but we are doing no good either. But, Kant argues, if we really respect others as moral agents, we will want to help them develop morally. Hence we have a duty to help, as well as not hinder, the moral development of others. This duty would involve at least a requirement to see that the basic physical needs of others are satisfied. To be moral a society must be more than just. Although there is no necessary connection between poverty and immorality, physical well-being is a necessary condition of complete perfection. A moral society must be benevolent as well as just.

Kant is certainly not a pure formalist in morals. Nevertheless Bradley is surely right in arguing that a purely formal ethics is hardly worth developing. We have seen that Kant's arguments gain greater plausibility and strength the richer their content becomes. Perhaps this explains why Bradley's attack on Kant was directed entirely at the principle of universalizability, and not at the principle of respect for persons.

The view that universal principles are a necessary component of moral thought implies the rejection of extreme forms of particularism, which deny that moral rules and principles have any role to play in moral thought. Bradley, like Kant, rejects radical particularism, because for him all thought proceeds by universals and never by particulars alone. Surely he is right on this point. As R. M. Hare has shown all particular moral judgements imply universal rules.[27] To deny the role of universal principles in moral thought is to deny a role for the principle of consistency. But if we abandon consistency, don't we abandon one of the necessary conditions of rationality? The minimum requirement for any rational system of morality is assent to the principle of universalizability. If we call something a good X, then we are committed to calling anything like it (something exactly similar or relevantly similar) good also. To say "X is good but Y which is relevantly similar to X, or exactly like X, is not good" is to express an inconsistency. To deny the principle of universalizability is to commit oneself to a form of moral irrationalism. To accept a central role for principles in moral thought makes the differences between Kant and Bradley less than is normally thought. Still there are major differences. Bradley, for example, thought that Kantian ethics was committed to a strict rule morality which made no allowances for the particular contexts in which we act:

> . . . is duty for duty's sake a valid
> formula, in the sense that we are to act
> always on a law and nothing but a law, and

that law can have no exceptions, in the
sense of particular cases where it is
over-ruled?[28]

Is it practically possible to follow a set of
absolute moral rules? Clearly not, for in most situations in which we find ourselves there are usually
several duties which conflict. When duties conflict what
am I to do? No matter what I do, I will be breaking an
absolute moral rule. Kant's formal principle of universalizability provides no solution to the problem of
moral dilemmas. Bradley thinks there are no moral rules,
except perhaps very vague general maxims ("do good and
avoid evil" or "do the best you can under the circumstances"), which cannot be broken on morally justifiable
grounds:

> There are few laws a breach of which (in
> obedience of a higher law) morality does
> not allow, and I believe there is none
> which is not to be broken in conceivable
> (imaginable) circumstances, though the
> necessity of deciding the question does
> not practically occur.[29]

Kant, according to Bradley, was wrong in trying to
establish absolute moral rules like "Lying is always
morally wrong" or "Suicide is always morally wrong," or
"Homicide is always morally wrong," or "Rebellion against
the state is always morally wrong," or "Disobedience in a
soldier is always morally wrong." Kant certainly had a
propensity for trying to establish moral absolutes but he
was too good a philosopher to make the simple mistakes
which idealists often attribute to him. Kant certainly

held that suicide is morally wrong but it is not clear
whether he held that it was <u>always</u> morally wrong. Kant
did hold that the rule against suicide expressed a
perfect duty to the self, which meant that no exceptions
were allowed on the basis of inclination. But then,
Bradley would agree with Kant that breaking a moral rule
simply because we feel inclined to do so is always
morally wrong. Bradley says:

> . . . you must never break a law of duty
> to please yourself, never for the sake of
> an end nor duty, but only for the sake of
> a superior and overruling duty."[30]

Kant also recognized that some actions considered to
be morally good are classed as cases of suicide (e.g.,
heroic, altruistic or honourable suicides, where persons
sacrifice their lives to save others), and that these
cases could be exceptions to the rule against suicide.
Kant sometimes argued that these actions are not cases of
suicide, because the basic intention of the agent is to
do some morally good action, and not to take his/her
life. But he also argued that these cases could be
accepted as suicides, but ones in which the duty to
preserve one's life was overridden by a stronger duty.
Kant never really made up his mind as to the correct way
to interpret these actions. In the <u>Metaphysical Princi-</u>
<u>ples of Morals</u>, he simply points to the different so-
lutions as problems in casuistry which perhaps limit any
system of moral rules. Kant asks:

> Is it self-murder to plunge oneself into
> certain death (like Curtius) in order to
> save one's country? Or is martyrdom--the

deliberate sacrifice of oneself for the good of mankind--also to be regarded, like the former case, as a heroic deed? Is committing suicide permitted in anticipation of an unjust death sentence from one's superior? Even if the sovereign permitted such a suicide (as Nero permitted of Seneca) . . .?[31]

Bradley agreed that the only valid reason for breaking a moral obligation is to avoid breaking a superior obligation. Nevertheless, he argued that there is no point in attempting to work out a complete and consistent set of moral rules which would show us our duty in every case. For Bradley no science of casuistry can solve moral dilemmas. Bradley's rejection of casuistry marks a radical departure from the ethical theories of both the Utilitarians and Kantians. In his critique of Sidgwick's utilitarianism Bradley points out that its objective is to produce a scientific casuistry:

The object or scope of the 'science' is practical. It is to direct us to 'externally' and 'objectively right' conduct. It is to tell us what to do, not merely in general, but in particular. It is to be no mere outline but a scientific code.[32]

The utilitarians conceive ethics as a practical discipline which should produce a scientific ethics which is applicable in real life. They believe the moral philosopher should guide his own behaviour by a code which provides a canon for every possible case. They are also obligated to enlighten others as to right and wrong conduct. What good is ethics if it has no practical use? Why bother studying it or paying ethicists to teach it in our universities, if it does not help us, and our society, to become morally better? Just as physical engineering is the ultimate goal of the natural scientist, so ethical or social engineering is the ultimate goal of the ethicist.[33] The utilitarians should be pleased with the recent revival of interest in practical ethics at the universities and throughout the community. The utilitarian moral expert might come into his own at last.

Bradley thinks that the utilitarian project of a scientific casuistry is wrong-headed from the start. The mistake they make in ethics is exactly like the one they made in logic. The utilitarians believed that logic should be directed towards the improvement of the art of thinking, and they also believed that ethics should be directed towards the improvement of moral reasoning:

> Just as logic has been perverted into the art of reasoning, so Ethics has been perverted into the art of Morality. They are twin delusions we shall consign, if we are wise, to a common grave.[34]

In both cases the utilitarians tried to develop a system of principles and rules, which, when mechanically applied, would guide us to correct logical and moral conclusions in every case. But both projects are futile, because you cannot produce a set of rules which will adequately grasp the infinite complexity of our logical and moral experience:

> Unless you artificially limit the facts, then models of reasoning cannot be

procured, since you would need in the end
an infinitude of schemes to parallel the
infinitude of possible relations. And a
code of morality is no less impossible.[35]

Bradley rejects all forms of casuistry. It makes no
difference whether it is based on the utilitarian principle of utility, or the Kantian principle of universalizability, or the religious principle of obedience to the
will of God. They are all equally unacceptable, because
they presuppose mechanistic methodologies, which cannot
capture the uniqueness of individual moral experience.[36]
In particular moral judgements you have to take into
account the total context:

Here we can refuse to consider no single
item of the whole complication. The
previous life of the man, his difference
from other men, the combination of circumstances in its general character and then
in relation to this man, all have to be
admitted in moral judgement.[37]

There can be no fruitful move directly from theory
to practise in ethics. And this is true for both the
deductive and inductive methods of standard logics.
Ethical theory, for Bradley, has no direct role to play
in practical ethics, hence Bradley is free of the charge
of confusing fact and value. Ethics does however have an
indirect role to play in practical ethics. Bradley's
views of practical ethics and logic are similar. Logic,
like ethics, has no direct contribution to make to
improving our thinking, but it can make an indirect
contribution. Logic as we saw can prevent us from using

inadequate mechanistic approaches to reasoning, and this may prevent us from making errors.[38]

The role Bradley assigns to theory when applied to practise is modest. It is negative only. The study of logic may prevent some errors but it does not develop our capacity for rational thought. It has no positive contribution to make to practical logic. Similarly ethical theory has a negative contribution to make to practical ethics. It can, for example, prevent us from embarking on the perilous and futile seas of casuistry. In avoiding these errors we could also avoid aiding and abetting immorality. Bradley thinks that most philosophers who defend systems of casuistry are well-intentioned, if a bit obtuse. They frequently share the same moral values as Bradley, the values of ordinary morality, and so do not present a danger to the moral community. But this may not be so when a sophisticated casuistry falls into the wrong hands:

> But once admit the principle, and what is
> to happen if men with no sense or hold on
> real life, but gifted with a logical
> faculty, begin systematically to deduce
> from this slippery principle? Is this not
> a danger, and is it wholly an imaginary
> danger?[39]

For Bradley, ethical theory has an important but largely negative contribution to make to practical morality. He was always skeptical about its capacity to help develop the individual, or society, morally. And so far as he goes, Bradley appears to be right. Recent work in applied ethics has shown that the mechanical application of ethical theories to solve particular moral dilemmas, e.g., in clinical settings, just doesn't work. A. L. Caplan has aptly dubbed this common approach to practical ethics "the engineering model":

> Having mastered the extant range of normative theories and moral traditions and armed with an understanding of deductive logic the applied ethicist is able to combine theory with empirical data to provide solutions to various moral quandaries which are raised by those persons concerned with practical affairs or public policy formulation.[39]

This is the same casuistry that Bradley rejected and for the same reasons, the complexity of particular experiences defeats it. Modern ethicists have also begun to recognize that applied ethics will only became fecund if it substitutes organic for mechanical theories of moral reasoning, a theoretical shift Bradley could certainly have approved of.[41] No science of casuistry then can solve our moral dilemmas because in the end circumstances would defeat it. We cannot produce a general formula for resolving moral dilemmas because the particular context in which an action is done will determine its morality. Particular moral judgements are intuitive according to Bradley, and are a function of unique persons acting in unique circumstances.

Bradley doesn't give us a very thorough analysis of what is involved in these intuitive judgements but nevertheless he holds that they are an important feature of our ordinary moral lives. In most ordinary ethical situations we rarely reflect on our principles, we rarely have them directly before our minds. Indeed we commonly believe that to look for reasons for all our conduct is pedantic or absurd. In fact it may be immoral to do so, for he who deliberates too long is usually lost. In particular situations we need to act and this involves the ability to size up the situation quickly, for example to recognize that a certain act is both a case of truth-telling and of harming an innocent person and to search for ways to express both values in our conduct. Moral judgement is a matter of insight, not the mechanical application of rules to particular cases. Theoretical intelligence does not guarantee that we shall judge moral issues correctly. Moral judgement is a function of personality and this is why the ordinary man can compete with the educated in matters of morals:

> Everyman has the morality he has made his own in his mind, and he 'sees' or 'feels' or 'judges' accordingly, though he does not reason explicitly from data to conclu-sion.[42]

Particular moral experience must have some episte-mological role to play in establishing, modifying or creating moral rules. In most cases our system of moral rules works adequately as a guide to conduct, but in difficult moral situations it often proves inadequate. The moral dilemma plays a central role in our lives because it arises out of our attempt to conduct ourselves in terms of a coherent system of morality. Indeed it is our assent to the moral rules which creates the dilemmas in the first place. If we did not hold that lying was morally wrong, and that harming others was morally wrong, then it would not matter if a certain action could be considered both a case of lying and of harming others.

Without assent to the rules there would be no moral dilemmas. Rules applied in a context then help us to identify when we are confronted with a moral dilemma but they don't always provide us with a solution to them. Consequently, rules do have a necessary role to play in moral thought, as Kant argued, but they must always be tested against particular moral experience. But what sort of test could this be? For Bradley there is a dialectical relation between the systems of moral rules which orders our conduct and the particular experiences which brings it into play. When we are faced with a moral dilemma something must change. We must give epistemological priority to either the system of rules or particular experience. The problem is to know which one should be chosen. Kantians would choose the system of rules over particular experiences. To solve moral dilemmas the rules need to be ranked, in terms of a single unifying principle. For the Kantian this is the principle of respect for persons, "always treat persons as ends-in-themselves never merely as a means." Although there is no doubt that the principle of respect for persons is a fundamental moral principle, these are other principles which appear to be equally fundamental, e.g., the principle of sanctity of life, or quality of life. So the choice of a final principal of morals is arbitrary, because we cannot select a first principle of morality without appeal to experience.

Utilitarians on the other hand would choose particular experiences over rules. Rules have practical priority over particular experiences but particular experiences have epistemological priority over rules. A well grounded particular judgement always takes precedence over a moral rule. Any moral rule ought to be broken, if doing so will produce a greater balance of pleasure over pain.

For Bradley neither answer does justice to our moral experience. Moral dilemmas are not merely intellectual puzzles, they are intrinsic to the moral life. It is the moral dilemma that provides the dynamics of moral development. Dilemmas introduce tension and discord into our lives. They are agonizing experiences, not merely intellectual annoyances. A son's mother is dying of cancer. Her condition is gross. She is hooked up to several life-saving machines. There are tubes going in and out of her body like long pale worms. She gurgles and croaks. Her eyes plead for mercy. She has said many times "I do not want to die like this." Should the son choose sanctity of life or quality of life? Should he honour her request for a dignified death? Does he help her die or does he let her live? He wants to rid himself of the anguish. He wants to end his mother's suffering; yet respect life. He is distraught. He needs to restore peace and harmony to his soul. He begins to understand that respect for life involves the acceptance of death. He pulls the plug and ties the tubes. He succours her. He allows her to die a dignified death. Death is an evil that has now lost its sting. His mother's life is properly completed. She dies with a smile on her face. The circle has closed. His own life is richer and more fully integrated. He has grown morally. He is a richer person for it, and he can continue to grow. Moral dilemmas are resolved by developing richer and more fully integrated personalities. Sometimes we grow by changing our conduct, sometimes by modifying our systems of morality. Most frequently we change both, because our systems of morality and our conduct are just different aspects of the same process, a developing moral agent. Without the dialectic between rules and particular experience there would be no moral growth because there would be no way by which we could learn from experience.

Kantianism certainly does a better job with moral agency than utilitarianism does. And it does not mistakenly reduce will to desire. A mistake which Edward Bond has shown is still perpetrated by a surprising number of our top rated moral philosophers.[43] The mistake is clothed in more logically ornate dress but it is still a serious mistake, as Bond amply demonstrates. Kantianism allows for the possibility of conscientious conduct, of doing something because we believe it is the right thing to do. It also gives a more satisfactory account than utilitarianism does, of the central role which moral rules play in moral experience. It also recognizes that guilt is a necessary condition of punishment. It does not turn punishment into therapy as utilitarianism does, so it is able to give a more complex account of the moral basis of the institutions of law and punishment. Finally it places the idea of the "good man" at center stage in the moral drama. For the Kantian the end for man is moral virtue. We are to act conscientiously. We are to do our duty because it is the right thing to do, and not to gain pleasure, or to avoid pain. So far so good, but again, for Bradley, not good enough. Kantianism proposes a theory of virtue, but not the right one. For the conscientious person, the central fact of the moral life is the struggle between will and desire, and virtue means the total suppression of desire:

> The 'ought' is the command of the formal
> will, and duty is the obedience or, more
> properly, the compulsion of the lower self
> by that will or the realization of the

form in and against the recalcitrant
matter of the desires.[44]

The pursuit of virtue apart from desire produces an
emotionally repressed person. Desire is the basic source
of evil for the Kantian. It is the devil who wants to
smash down the rational doors of the will, and unleash
the fury of its irrationality on the ego. It seems to me
that Bradley is correct on this point. Kant did not
ignore the virtue of benevolence, but he clearly mis-
trusted desire. Take sexual desire, for example.[45] Kant
believed that the pursuit of sexual pleasure independent
of the natural purpose of procreation was immoral. Sex
for pleasure's sake is also inconsistent with self-
respect. According to Kant we have no right to make use
of another person for sexual pleasure without their
consent. Rape is clearly inconsistent with respect for
others as moral agents. Bradley would accept all this.
But Kant also believed we have a duty to ourselves not to
pursue sex for pleasure's sake. The moral man does not
lust. Lusting is morally worse than attempting suicide.
Kant says:

> The obstinate throwing away of one's life
> as a burden is at least not a weak surren-
> der to animal pleasure, but requires
> courage; and where there is courage, there
> is always respect for the humanity in
> one's own person. On the other hand, when
> one abandons himself entirely to an animal
> inclination, he makes himself an object of
> unnatural gratification, i.e., a loathsome
> thing, and thus deprives himself of all
> self-respect.[46]

It takes guts to commit suicide, but to give in to lust is to display gross moral weakness. Bradley would agree that the pursuit of sexual pleasure merely for sexual gratification is immoral. Sex is normally an interpersonal relationship, and so sexual pleasure, if it is to be morally valid, must be an aspect of that relationship. Lust is the characteristic vice of the voluptuary, and so the sexual voluptuary is not likely to find satisfaction. So far so good, but, again, not good enough. There is no reason for assuming, as Kant does, that it takes more courage to cope with violence than it does to cope with our sexual desires. Nor is it clear that the principle of respect for persons is inconsistent with respecting ourselves and others as sexual beings. The will for Kant might be a gentle master, working as it does through rationality, dignity, and respect for persons, nevertheless it is, or ought to be, the matter.

The function of will for Kant is to subjugate desire. Moral weakness is seen simply as weakness of will for which there is no excuse. We are totally responsible for our conduct. For Kantianism the idea of diminished responsibility would make little sense. The origin of evil is to be found in the human soul, not in society. For the utilitarian the exact opposite would be true. Since will is merely the expression of the strongest desire, then weakness of will is simply a case of bad conditioning. Society has programmed the person to want the wrong thing. No one is really responsible for anything they do. The origin of evil is to be found in society and not in the human soul. Kantianism eliminates desire and excuses, utilitarianism eliminates reason and responsibility. But for Bradley neither of these views gives a satisfactory account of moral weakness. We do recognize the existence of moral weakness, and other excuses, and so we accept the concept of "diminished responsibility." We understand that we are indeed human. That is why mercy and compassion are allowed to override justice in certain cases. It is also the reason why Bradley believes that we can't accept a purely retributive view of punishment:

> But then this retributive view pure and simple will not work. For practise, if taken by itself, it is too narrow, and even in itself it labours under intrinsic difficulties.[47]

In practise it is not always that easy to distinguish between "willful badness" and "unwilled disease."[48] Each person is a complex developing whole in which will and desire are organically related. For Bradley the function of will is to bring the disparate elements of the soul into harmony with each another. We have several choices in the way we relate will and desire. We can repress our desires as the Kantian recommends. We can ignore will altogether as the utilitarian recommends. Or we can try to make will and desire function as a harmonious system, as Bradley recommends. For the Kantian, moral weakness is lack of will power, for the utilitarian, it is a matter of a weak desire to do good. For the idealist moral weakness is a structural problem in personality development which inhibits healthy growth. Evil for Bradley is simultaneously a product of both society and the human soul. Any natural desire can be moralized, according to Bradley: "I do not know any inborn propensity which may not be moralized into good or turned into bad."[49] If we examine the virtues or vices of any man we can see that the natural basis of every virtue might under certain conditions have been developed into a vice and the natural basis of every vice into a virtue. Take sexual desire for example.[50] It is obvious that sexual desire in itself is not intrinsically evil, it is just part of the human condition. Sexual desire can be turned into something good or evil. It forms the root of some of the greatest of human virtues, the good lover and the devoted spouse, as it does some of the greatest of human vices, the sexual violence of the rapist and the extraordinary cruelty of the sexual sadist. To conquer sexual violence and cruelty we need to integrate sexual desires with our other desires, rather than trying to spike them out with the sadistic heel of fear or entombing them within a guilty conscience.

Bradley has shown that utilitarianism and Kantianism do not do justice to the facts of our moral experience. Both theories are inadequate. It remains for Bradley to demonstrate that his Ethical Idealism can do justice to the facts.

NOTES

Chapter III: Kantian Moral Psychology

1   Kant, The Critique of Pure Reason, translated by Norman Kemp Smith (Macmillan, London, 1929), pp. 328-384.

2   F. H. Bradley, Ethical Studies, p. 143.

3   F. H. Bradley, Ibid., p. 11.

4   F. H. Bradley, Ibid., p. 12.

5   F. H. Bradley, Ibid., p. 148.

6   F. H. Bradley, Ibid., p. 148.

7   F. H. Bradley, Ibid., p. 142, footnote 2, and p. 148, footnote 1.

8   D. Hume, Enquiries Concerning the Principles of Morals (ed. by L. A. Selby-Bigge, Oxford, 1893, revised by P. H. Nidditch, Oxford, 1975), p. 172; cf. J. S. Mill, Utilitarianism, p. 239, "Will is the child of desire. . . ."

9   Kant, Ethical Philosophy (The Grounding For a Metaphysics of Morals, Hackett, Indianapolis, 1983), p. 30.

10 Cf. R. M. Hare, Freedom and Reason (Oxford, 1963), pp. 10-16.

11 Kant, Ethical Philosophy (The Grounding), p. 36.

12 Cf., Alan Donagan, The Theory of Morality (Chicago, 1977), and R. S. Downie and E. Telfer, Respect for Persons (Allen and Unwin, London, 1969), for the best modern versions of the theory.

13 Kant, Ethical Philosophy (The Grounding), p. 30. Cf. my The Moral Question: Ethical Theory (TV Ontario, 1982), pp. 31-36, for fuller account of Kant's moral philosophy.

14 Kant, Ibid., p. 30.

15 Kant, Ibid., pp. 36-37, and Ethical Philosophy (The Metaphysics of Morals), pp. 82-85.

16 Kant, Ibid., p. 31.

17 Kant, Ethical Philosophy (The Grounding), p. 37, and Ethical Philosophy (The Metaphysics of Morals), pp. 108-111.

18 Kant, Ibid., p. 31.

19 Kant, Ibid., p. 31.

20 Cf. M. G. Singer, Generalization in Ethics (New York, Knopf, 1961).

21 Cf., J. L. Austin, How to do Things with Words (Oxford, 1962); J. Rawls, "Two Concepts of Rules," Philosophical Review (Volume LXIV, 1954), pp. 3-52; and J. R. Searle, "How to derive 'ought' from 'is'," The Is Ought Question (MacMillan, 1969), pp. 120-134 and pp. 259-271.

22 R. M. Hare, "The Promising Game," The Is Ought Question, pp. 144-156.

23 Kant, Ethical Philosophy, p. 37.

24 Kant, Ibid., p. 32.

25 R. M. Hare, Freedom and Reason, pp. 104-106 and pp. 157-185.

26 Kant, Ethical Philosophy, p. 27 and pp. 112-141.

27 R. M. Hare, Freedom and Reason, pp. 10-16. Hare's theory of moral reasoning represents the best modern attempt to develop ethics on the basis of the principle of universalizability. But because he sharply divides the form from the content of moral reasoning his account of moral thought is incomplete. Cf. my article, "Hare's Universal Prescriptivism," Dialogue (Volume III, 1964, No. 2), pp. 191ff.

28 F. H. Bradley, Ethical Studies, p. 156.

29 F. H. Bradley, Ibid., p. 157.

30 F. H. Bradley, Ibid., p. 158.

31 Kant, Ethical Philosophy (Metaphysics of Morals), pp. 84-85.

32 F. H. Bradley, Collected Essays, p. 104.

33 F. H. Bradley, Principles of Logic, pp. 269-270.

34 F. H. Bradley, Ibid., p. 269.

35 F. H. Bradley, Ibid., p. 270.

36 F. H. Bradley, Collected Essays, p. 107.

37 F. H. Bradley, Ibid., p. 106.

38 See Chapter 1, p. 24.

39 F. H. Bradley, Collected Essays, p. 116.

40 A. L. Caplan, "Mechanics on Duty: The Limitations of a Technical Definition of Moral Expertise for Work in Applied Ethics," Canadian Journal of Philosophy (Supp. Volume VII, 1982), pp. 1-18; and C. N. Noble, "Ethics and Experts," Working Papers (July/August, 1980), pp. 57-60.

41 T. F. Ackerman, "What Bioethics Should Be," The Journal of Medicine and Philosophy (Volume V, No. 3), pp. 260-275.

42 F. H. Bradley, Ethical Studies, p. 196.

43 E. J. Bond, Reason and Value (Cambridge, 1983).

44 F. H. Bradley, Ethical Studies, p. 147.

45 Kant, Ethical Philosophy (The Metaphysics of Morals), pp. 85-88.

46 Kant, Ibid., p. 87.

47 F. H. Bradley, "Some Remarks on Punishment," Collected Essays, pp. 153-154.

48 F. H. Bradley, Ibid., p. 154.

49 F. H. Bradley, Ethical Studies, p. 278.

50 F. H. Bradley, Ibid., p. 279.

CHAPTER IV
Self-Realization and Egoism

For Bradley the good for man is "self-realization." The basic moral prescription of ethical idealism is "Realize oneself as a harmonious personality!" This bare hypothesis needs to be flushed out before it can be fully understood and substantiated by the facts of moral experience:

> All we know at present is that we are to realize the self as a whole; but as to what whole it is, we know nothing and must further consider.[1]

To understand the idea of self-realization we need first to understand the view of human nature which it presupposes. Ethical idealism is based on psychological idealism, the hypothesis that everyone can only realize self:

> . . . what we do do, is, perfectly or imperfectly, to realize ourselves, and that we cannot possibly do anything else; that all we can realize is (accident apart) our ends, or the objects we desire; and that all we can desire is, in a word, self.[2]

This thesis, as Bradley admits, could be accepted by the utilitarians, because "psychological idealism" bears a striking resemblance to their doctrine of "psychological egoism," i.e., "everyone can only act selfishly or in their self-interest."[3] Psychological egoism is the theoretical foundation for both ethical egoism, "everyone ought to act selfishly or everyone ought to pursue his/her self-interest," and classical utilitarianism "everyone ought to pursue the greatest happiness of the greatest number." If psychological idealism is merely a form of psychological egoism then Bradley is in double trouble, because his idealism would be based on a psychology he thought was false, and which sustained an ethical theory he despised. It is very important for Bradley to be able to distinguish clearly between psychological egoism and psychological idealism. How do the doctrines differ from each other, and why is the former unacceptable and the latter acceptable?

In utilitarian psychology, Bradley argues, we aim at states of our own being, hence man is a selfish creature who can only pursue his own pleasure:

> If we could accept the theory that the end or motive is always the idea of a pleasure (or pain) of our own, which is associated with the object presented, and which is that in the object which moves us, and the only thing which does move us, then from such a view it would follow at once that all we can aim at is a state of ourselves. We cannot, however, accept the theory, since we believe it both to ignore and to be contrary to fact. [4]

Utilitarianism maintains a kind of psychological solipsism, which implies that everyone can only act selfishly and this view, that man is naturally selfish, is untenable. The selfish view of man is false, first because it implies that no genuine act of self-sacrifice is possible:

> Can I sacrifice myself? Oh yes, I can like what others do not like, and the result may prove painful to myself and pleasant to others; but so it may be with the result of any other act: or the result may be pleasant to me, though it would not be so to others. And so self-sacrifice is a peculiar sort of self-seeking, arising from mistaken notions or eccentric tastes.[5]

But people do sacrifice themselves for the good of others. We have our genuine saints and heroes, hence the claim that man is naturally selfish, and is incapable of self-sacrifice, is false. The theory also implies that genuine benevolence is impossible. But again people do act benevolently or altruistically. Someone intervenes to prevent a serious assault from occurring. Not everyone stands around watching impassively as others are maimed or murdered. The theory also implies that people never do anything because they believe it is morally right. But again some people are conscientious. A bank clerk prevents a robbery because he believes it is his duty to do so. But the egoist will argue that he really did it for the praise, and perhaps the raise, he would receive from his boss. Suppose the teller denies that he had any such ulterior motives? For the egoist he must be lying, deceiving himself, or be unaware of his true motives for doing what he did. But why should the teller accept the egoist's explanation of his behaviour? Surely he knows as much about himself as an outside observer does? It may sometimes be true that others understand us better than we understand ourselves, but surely this is not always the case. Normally the agent knows why he does the things he does, and he would consider the egoist's analysis inappropriate, and presumptuous:

> He believes that we are trying to persuade him that he and others seek the good and avoid the bad, in all cases, with an ulterior object--as a means, that is to say, to something else which is the end: and this idea he indignantly repudiates. He considers our question of the motive an idle triviality, because asking what everybody knows; or an attempt to mislead, because presupposing what is palpably false.[6]

There is no reason to accept the egoist's theory of knowledge of other minds which implies that an observer's explanation of our behaviour is always superior to our own. A psychologist who looks at persons as if they were objects will be in a very poor position to understand others. Persons are not merely more complex forms of stones. If he/she looks at them as persons his/her science will have to take a humbler approach towards them. He/she will have to view them as autonomous moral agents who have dignity and rights. The object of his/her science will no longer be power, control and manipulation but understanding, respect and the development of the other as a free being. Psychological egoism also implies determinism and since determinism erases moral responsibility and respect it is inconsistent with any ethics.[7]

To save psychological egoism utilitarian theorists have used a number of strategies. The most common, dating back to Hobbes, is to make the theory into a form of rational egoism. This revision states that although everyone can only pursue his/her own self-interest, the agent is free to choose the means to that end. The theory of rational self-interest is, as Hobbes recognized, much stronger than the original version of egoism. It even allows for limited freedom. It implies only partial determinism. The ultimate goal of all human action is determined, but the means to that goal are not. It also allows for a kind of benevolence and conscientiousness. However they can only be chosen as a means to self-interest and never for their own sake. Genuine benevolence and conscientiousness are ruled out by the theory. But again this is counter-factual. There do exist people of pure benevolence and those who behave purely for the sake of duty. So even the revised form of psychological egoism cannot account for the full range of human conduct.

Rational egoism also tends to become trivial. Its defenders stretch the meaning of "self-interest" to include genuine benevolence, and conscientiousness. Everything we do, including ignoring our self-interest, becomes a form of self-interest. Imprudence is as inexplicable in terms of the theory as benevolence is. But again there are people who act intentionally against their own best interests. The smoker who knows tobacco is a carcinogen, but who refuses to stop smoking is such a case. Again the psychological egoist may search for further evidence that real imprudence doesn't exist. The smoker doesn't really believe smoking causes cancer or if he does, there are other interests, like pleasing friends and peers, which would account for it. But this too is to bring everything, including the opposite of self-interest, under the same net. According to Bradley when pushed far enough "psychological egoism" becomes indistinguishable from "tautological egoism":

> If selfishness is self-seeking, and to seek self is never to act apart from desire and our desire, never to do anything but what we want, then surely all deliberate actions must be considered selfish. For deliberately to act without an object in view is impossible; duty is done for duty's sake only when duty is an object of desire; thought as such does not move; and only the thought of what you like or dislike brings with it a practical result. Whether we consider blind appetite, or conscious desire or circumspect volition, the result is the same. No act is ever without a reason for its existence, and the reason is always a feeling of pain or of pleasure or of both. We seek what we like, and avoid what we dislike; we do what we want and this is selfish.[8]

Which is to say, 'I do what I want to do,' or 'I do what I do.' It is to express a trivial tautology. It is to reject what was intrinsically interesting about the doctrine of psychological egoism in the first place, i.e., the explanation of all human behaviour in terms of selfishness. The theory at this point ceases to have any interesting explanatory powers.

A second strategy, adopted by Mill, was to accept the existence of benevolent and conscientious behaviour but argue that these facts can be explained in terms of association psychology.[9] Psychological egoism could be saved by producing a genetic psychology which explains the development of non-selfish conduct out of the narcissistic hedonism of childhood. Mill believed that conscience is acquired and is not innate as Kant, and other rationalists, believed. Kant says:

> Just so, conscience is not something to be acquired, and there is no duty to provide oneself with a conscience; but in so far as every man is a moral being, he has it originally within him.[10]

The idea that morality is learned was extremely important for utilitarians like Mill, because it implied that humankind was capable of moral progress. If conscience is innate there would be no place for social reform or moral education. However, if conscience is acquired then the progressive improvement of humankind becomes a real possibility. Mill holds that conscience is a mechanism of social control, and not a capacity for distinguishing right from wrong, as Kantians believe.[11] Our sense of duty, according to Mill, is primarily attached to customary morality, the set of rules and attitudes which have been inculcated by the social groups which reared us. Conscience is a product of social conditioning. The human conscience originally is moulded entirely by the society and not the individual. It is a moral tabula rasa which can be imprinted in any way society desires. Mill says:

> Unhappily it is also susceptible, by a
> sufficient use of the external sanctions
> and of the force of early impressions, of
> being cultivated in almost any direction,
> so that there is hardly anything so absurd
> or so mischievous that it may not, by
> means of these influences, be made to act
> on the human mind with all the authority
> of conscience.[12]

Conscience is created by turning external motives into internal ones. A child does X and as a result he receives a pleasant sensation from things and/or persons in his environment. A child does Y and as a result he receives an unpleasant or painful sensation from things and/or persons in his environment. If this continues to happen, whenever the child does X or Y, then X becomes associated with pleasure, and Y with pain. The twin processes of positive and negative reinforcement create a habitual tendency in the child to desire X and to be averse to Y. Of course the child only desires X because it is a means to pleasure, and is averse to Y because it causes pain. X is only instrumentally and not intrinsically good, and Y is only instrumentally and not intrinsically bad. The theory has so far not been able to explain the origin of conscientiousness. To achieve this something more is required. Mill thought that his doctrine of acquired ends-in-themselves could accomplish this.[13] Mill, as we saw, admitted that it is obvious that people pursue ends different from pleasure and one such end is virtue:

> Now it is palpable that they do desire
> things which, in common language, are

> decidedly distinguished from happiness.
> They desire, for example, virtue and the
> absence of vice, no less really than
> pleasure and the absence of pain. The
> desire of virtue is not as universal, but
> it is as authentic a fact as the desire of
> happiness.[14]

He explains this fact by arguing that virtue is an acquired end-in-itself. At first we pursue virtue as a means to pleasure. If we act virtuously we receive pleasure from others who reward our good behaviour. After a long period of associating virtue and pleasure the two become cemented together and we come to pursue it for its own sake. Like Pavlovian dogs we salivate when the bell rings, not when dinner appears. Virtue now functions as an autonomous end, and not simply as a means to pleasure. Virtue is like power. At first we want it for what we can get with it. But later we come to desire it for its own sake. We want as much of it as we can get, even if we don't need it:

> Virtue, according to the utilitarian
> conception, is a good of this description.
> There was no original desire of it, or
> motive to it, save its conduciveness to
> pleasure, and especially to protection
> from pain. But through its association
> thus formed it may be felt a good-in-
> itself, and desired as such with as great
> intensity as any other good. . . .[15]

The doctrine of "acquired ends-in-themselves" is deceptive. It appears to raise virtue and conscientiousness to the level of intrinsic value, but in reality, it never does. The only intrinsic good in the system is still pleasure, not virtue. Means and end are still externally and not internally related. Virtue and pleasure are merely pasted to-gether and when the glue ages they fall apart. Bradley does not deny that the virtue is pleasant nor that pleasure is good. What he rejects is the view that they are mechanically related to each other. For Bradley pleasure and virtue are internally related. They are different aspects of a complex psychological whole. If we hold to the mechanical view then we will be unable to explain the development of the moral agent from its narcissistic beginnings in childhood. A rational autonomous agent thinks and acts on moral principles. He/she is self-legislating. He/she takes responsibility for what he/she does. He/she is capable of acting in terms of disinterested principles like fairness and respect for others as persons. These principles imply the capacity to be impartial when this attitude is appropriate. True conscientiousness will never emerge on the basis of the laws of association. And it's no use trying to bridge the gap between interested and disinterested conduct via the concept of sympathy, as Mill and other utilitarians try to do.[16] It may be true that we naturally delight in the happiness of others and suffer from their unhappiness. "Taken broadly, it is true that the idea of other's pleasure or pain must be pleasant or painful to my mind."[17] This sympathetic capacity is also a major source of our benevolence towards others:

> It is true that I am led to promote or
> remove this source of my feelings and it
> is true that, in the main, I do so by a
> benefit to the person concerned.[18]

And lack of sympathy is a major source of our
immorality towards others. But, Bradley argues, concern
is also a source of sympathy: "Instead of saying that
interest comes from sympathy we might say that sympathy
depends on interest."[19] He argues that expressions of
pleasure in others tend to evoke pleasure in us. A
smiling person tends to make us smile. Expressions of
pain in others tend to produce pain in us. A crying
person tends to sadden us. But Bradley points out we can
have these primitive sympathetic responses and still have
no desire to alter the situation of others. Indeed we
could desire just the opposite, hence sympathy could also
be a source of immorality. I might do harm to others,
the sight of whom gives me pain. Sympathy does not
automatically produce concern for the welfare of others.
Not only can we have sympathy without benefit, we can
have concern without sympathy. Certainly sympathy is no
part of our concern for ourselves, for inanimate objects,
or for non-sentient living things like trees or flowers:

> We are sorry when we see the daisies mown
> or the trees cut down, and we take an
> interest in many inanimate objects. But
> do we sympathize? For trees and flowers
> we to some extent feel, but can most of us
> feel for a book or a house?[20]

We might think the case with animals and mankind are
different. We are concerned about animal welfare because

we sympathize with their feelings of pleasure and pain. But this does not by itself explain people's attitude towards animals. Understanding that animals suffer is perhaps a necessary condition for concern about their welfare but it is not a sufficient condition. Many people realize that animals suffer but they do not concern themselves with their welfare. Some people abuse their pets because their pain reactions amuse them. "Just look at him jump!" Experimenters who use animals in analgesic research know that their subjects suffer. If animals did not feel pain the research would be pointless. To ensure our safety we require that all drugs be tested on animals first. Where then is our concern for the welfare of animals? Moral thought needs more than an appeal to our natural sentiment of sympathy to be effective:

> . . . it is clear that in sympathy we have not got the whole of morality. If it is right to affirm, without sympathy no interest, it is as right to affirm, without interest no sympathy. I believe neither would be accurate.

Bradley does not deny that humans are sympathetic creatures. But he does deny that sympathy works by putting ourselves in the shoes of others, and imagining their pleasures and pains were ours. Sympathy does not work in this mechanistic, egoistic way. Our involvement with others is more profound than association psychology allows. If you start with psychological egoism you will end up with psychological egoism, and you will never be able to explain the emergence of the moral agent, no matter how you twist the so-called laws of association.

To explain the fact of moral agency a different psychology is required.

Since psychological egoism is untenable, it is important for Bradley to show that his doctrine of self-realization cannot be reduced to it. This is difficult to do because he also holds that what we desire is always ourselves in some form or other:

> . . . though we do not admit that the motive is always, or in most cases, the idea of a state of our feeling self, yet we think it is clear that nothing moves unless it be desired, and that what is desired is ourself.[22]

Nevertheless self-realization does not reduce to selfishness, because the relationship between ourselves and others is not one of hedonistic narcissism. Rather it is a form of deep personal identification with them. Without others we could not fully be ourselves. We need others in order to understand both what we are and what we are not. We need others in order to grow. Unless we can imagine what we are not, we wouldn't be able to make ourselves into what we ought to be:

> The essence of desire for an object would thus be the feeling of our affirmation in the idea of something not ourself, felt against the feeling of ourself as, without the object, void and negated; and it is the tension of this relation which produces motion. If so, then nothing is desired except that which is identified with ourselves, and we can aim at nothing,

except so far as we aim at ourselves in
it.[23]

What we want is a state of ourselves, but this is quite different from maintaining that what we want is our own pleasure, or what is associated with our pleasure. Human desire, according to Bradley, is governed by an entirely different set of laws than those proposed by the utilitarian psychologists. What are these laws? The basic law which governs the whole of our mental life is The Law of Individuation:

> Every mental element (to use a metaphor) strives to make itself a whole or to lose itself in one, and it will not have its company assigned to it by mere conjunction in presentation.[24]

Bradley could have called it the law of organic wholes, because all mental processes tend to develop as integrated unities. We have a primitive drive to develop as organic wholes, to structure our experience, to give it order and meaning, to make it more homogenous and comprehensive, yet unique. The law of individuation is a dynamic law, one which governs our mental development and the growth of our personalities. The law of individuation is at work in all mental processes; perception, thought, feeling, and will:

> I am contented with the view that for psychology the law of individuation is an ultimate, and this law succeeded, because it answers to external events in a way which to psychology is itself once more an

ultimate; and that, thus succeeding, it becomes an end and a standard for thought and feeling and will, according to the special conditions of these processes.[25]

In perception, the principle operates in terms of two secondary laws, The Law of Contiguity or Reintegration: "Every mental element when present tends to reinstate those elements with which it has been presented,"[26] and The Law of Fusion or Coalescence or Blending: "Where different elements (or relations of elements) have any feature the same they may unite wholly or partially."[27] These two secondary laws reappear in different ways in thought, feeling and will. For thought they are the principles of consistency and completeness, which together make up the coherence theory of truth:

Truth is an ideal expression of the Universe, at once coherent and comprehensive. It must not conflict with itself, and there must be no suggestion which fails to fall inside it. Perfect truth in short must realize the idea of a systematic whole. And such a whole, we saw, possessed essentially the two characters of coherence and comprehensiveness.[28]

The two secondary laws represent different aspects of a single unified process. You cannot be coherent without being comprehensive. The search for coherence forces us to the comprehensive.[29] In pleasure, desire, and will, they reappear as harmony and growth: "The conditions of pleasure can, I think, be reduced to harmony (including pureness) and expansion, answering to consistency and completeness in knowledge."[30] Physical pleasure and physical pain are intrinsically connected to the physical well-being and ill-being of the agent.[31] Pleasure is a sign that an experience, or activity, is physically beneficial to the agent. Pain is a sign that an experience, or activity, is physically injurious to the agent. As a criterion for distinguishing benefit from harm, pleasure and pain have limited validity. They indicate only what is immediately good, or bad, as when water satisfies our thirst, or fire burns our skin. But pleasure can also disguise long-range threats, as the satisfaction derived from smoking tobacco or marijuana does. And pain disguises long-range benefits, as the discomfort of medical treatment sometimes does. The signals which physical pleasure and pain send to the agent are simple. The agent receives them and responds. They give no hint as to why an experience is beneficial or harmful for the agent. They express no general principle or criterion. They are like stop and go signs controlling city traffic. Mental pleasures and pains, on the other hand, present a more complex picture. The two conditions which appear to control mental pleasure, over and above its natural capacity as a sign that an activity is beneficial for the agent, are harmony and expansion (growth). The main conditions which appear to control mental pain, over and above its natural capacity as a sign that an activity is harmful for the agent, are discord, and attrition (failure to grow): "I will begin the inquiry from the side of pain. There it seems to me that discord is the one constant feature."[32] The essence of discord is unresolved tension, which arises when growth is frustrated. The loss of a loved one is not just unfelt absence, but felt absence:

> Wherever we have pains whose origin does
> not seem physical, there we find a colli-
> sion and a struggle of elements; and
> wherever we make a collision which is not
> rapidly arranged or subordinated, there we
> can always find pain. [33]

Bradley thinks it possible that the underlying principle of tension may explain physical as well as mental pain, but the final evidence for this would have to be supplied by physiology and not psychology. If discord and attrition are the basic characteristics of pain, harmony and growth are the basic characteristics of pleasure. Does this mean that pleasure is merely pain's alter ego? Is pleasure basically the removal of discord and tension? If this were the case, pleasure could be described in terms of expansion alone, and harmony would be reduced to the process of removing discord. For Bradley this will not do. Pleasure is a positive, as well as a negative, state of affairs, and harmony by itself produces pleasure:

> Pleasure thus will be the result of such
> positive conditions as imply the absence
> of pain. . . . The absence of hindrance
> does not constitute the pleasure, pleasure
> is essentially positive. . . . [34]

It is unresolved tension which moves us to rid ourselves of mental pain. We need to restore harmony and we can do this only by realizing ourselves. Pleasure then is not simply the absence of pain, but is also the good feeling, which accompanies successful self-reali-zation. Pleasure incorporates the two conditions of

harmony and expansion. These principles also underlie
desire, the mental process through which pleasure and
pain become related to the agent's conduct, and not just
his/her appetitive responses.

The first thing to understand about desire, according to Bradley, is that it is not merely pleasure and
pain: "Pleasure and Pain are not desire, nor does either
of them necessarily involve it."[35] Since we can experience sensations of pleasure and pain without an accompanying desire, neither can be equated to desire or aversion. Bradley cites the examples of the pleasures of
repose, or smell, as instances of pleasurable experiences
that are not accompanied by desire. He cites the example
of dull constant pain, as an instance of painful experience that is not accompanied by aversion. In the latter
case, Bradley points out that although the experience
would be accompanied by restlessness, it wouldn't follow
that a desire for change would necessarily arise. Nor
could we claim that pain always produces tension and
hence desire for change. Although desire certainly
involves tension, tension is not the whole of desire.
And we shouldn't think that desire is simply the anticipation of pleasure because, as we saw, pleasure is
not always the object of desire. To make this mistake is
to lay the groundwork for a greater mistake, the identification of the pleasant with the desirable (a mistake
common to many utilitarians). Nevertheless pleasure and
pain are not accidental for desire:

> Thus for desire we must have three ele-
> ments--an idea conflicting with reality,
> that idea felt to be pleasant, and the
> reality felt to be painful;, and these

elements felt as one whole state make up
desire.[36]

In desire there is always a mental feature which is
out of step with existence, hence the principle of
harmony will govern the development of desire, as it does
pleasure and pain. The principle of growth will also be
relevant to desire, because to fulfil desires is to
realize self, and to realize oneself is to grow. Desire
is a complex mental state that involves three components,
a goal to be realized, that goal felt as pleasant, and
present reality felt to be painful. Desire is not just
the anticipation of pleasure as the utilitarians believe.
Present discomfort or pain is as important in desire as
anticipated pleasure. As with mental pleasure/pain, it
is unresolved tension, discomfort or dissatisfaction,
which turns wishing into wanting, which moves the agent
to try to fulfil his desire. We need to restore harmony
and we can do this only by acting. Through acting we
develop towards greater individuation, to more complex
states of personality that are marked by greater richness, integration, and uniqueness.

Bradley's theory of desire is clearly different from
that developed by the psychological egoists. It is more
complex, and the need for harmony is basic to it rather
than the desire for pleasure. Still, his theory of
desire is not sufficient to distinguish psychological
idealism and egoism. To do this Bradley needs to deal
with the problem of will. One of the weaknesses of
psychological egoism is its tendency to become trivial.
It tries to gather all explanation of behaviour under a
single umbrella. Not to have a desire to do something
becomes the same as saying there is no explanation for
the behaviour. An "unwanted action" becomes logically

equivalent to an "uncaused event." It is self-contradictory. It is analytically, or necessarily, false. But if this were the case, the theory would have to show that all acts of will were disguised forms of desire. The theory implies that we can never do what we don't want to do. We can never do our duty because it is our duty. We can never do anything because we believe it is the right thing to do. We can never act conscientiously. We can never do what is right, protect the innocent or defenceless from violence, for example, even if we don't feel like doing it. We can never act rationally, for acting conscientiously is a form of acting rationally, i.e., acting in accordance with principles. Hobbes had defined will as the strongest present desire. Hume thought that reason could not move us to action. In effect the utilitarian tradition in psychology denied the possibility of practical reason and moral freedom. Mill and Bain made some attempts to save the idea of practical reason by introducing a cognitive element into desire, the idea of the amount of pleasure and pain associated with our goals. This, however, is inadequate, because desire is seldom a desire for pleasure as such. If Bradley was to avoid this mistake he had to find a place in his psychology for a will which did not reduce to desire. The essence of will is, as Bradley recognizes, an idea producing its own existence through human agency:

> It is will when an idea produces its existence. A feature in present existence, not in harmony with that and working apart from it, gives itself another existence in which it is realized and where it is both idea and fact.[37]

The will is not a mysterious force which falls
outside the explanatory power of Idealist psychology.
Its control over human conduct can be explained by the
same fundamental law, The Law of Individuation:

> And Will is not a faculty or separate kind
> of phenomena. It is merely one special
> result of general laws and conditions, the
> main law of Individuation with its branch-
> es, Blending and Contiguity (Reinte-
> gration).[38]

Bradley, when he wrote Ethical Studies, appeared to
think, like the Utilitarians, that desire was essential
to volition, but his final position in the Collected
Essays was different:

> I cannot accept the doctrine that desire
> is essential to will. Where volition
> follows on a suggestion and follows
> without delay, to assume that desire in
> any proper sense must invariably be
> present seems plainly indefensible.[39]

Moral thinking can be used to explain conduct
without reference to desire or pleasure. The will, like
thought, is governed by the law of individuation, it just
expresses itself differently:

> The end of both is individuality, self-
> realization as the unity of harmony and
> expansion; but for will this must seek
> existence in the series of events. My end
> is to realize this perfection in my

> physical being, yet not in mine looked at
> by itself, but regarded as an element in a
> higher system. And, as with thought,
> harmony and expansion fall under one head,
> so it is again with will. If positive
> self-realization is the end and is essen-
> tial, that end, given plurality, becomes
> negative of discord. It means a harmoni-
> ous individuality that, because it finds
> opposition, is forced to expand.[40]

For the will it is the internal conflict between it and desire, or between conflicting obligations, which supply the dynamics of moral growth. Once more we seek to attain, both in our moral thought and conduct, a larger unity which contains greater richness, and unique-ness. Desire, thought, and will, are distinct processes of the human mind which cannot be reduced to each other, but whose functioning can be understood in terms of the same general psychological laws. These general laws provide more adequate accounts of the phenomena of appetite, desire, thought and will than the laws of association do. They also give a better account of our moral experience. They help explain, for example, the moral struggle more satisfactorily than its rivals do.

The moral struggle, Bradley suggests, is an impor-tant fact of the moral life and any theory of morality must give an adequate account of it. At one time or another in our lives most of us have had the experience of an inner struggle, which seems to be a war between two different selves, one which is identified with everything that is good in us, and another which seems to be iden-tified with everything that is bad in us. We recognize both of these selves to be part of us, but they seem so different from one another that when we are good, and when we are bad, we seem not to be quite the same person:

> I feel at times identified with the good, as though all my self were in it; there are certain good habits and pursuits and companies which are natural to me, and in which I feel at home. And then again there are certain bad habits and pursuits and companies in which perhaps I feel no less at home, in which also I feel myself to be myself; and I feel that, when I am good and when I am bad I am not the same man but quite different and the world to the one self seems quite another thing to what it does to the other.[41]

These two selves do not present themselves as mere collections of desires and habits, some of which we call good, and some of which we call bad. But rather each seems to represent an active center within us. We actually experience them as two selves which struggle with each other. No doubt, as Bradley says, this description of the moral struggle, as a war between two different selves which struggle within us, is an exaggeration, if taken as a description for everyone. Still it is sufficiently accurate to describe a common psychological experience which in its abnormal forms develops into the problem of multiple personalities. What are the good and the bad selves? How do we distinguish between them? Bradley needs to provide answers to these questions if his moral psychology is to provide an acceptable account of the moral struggle. The good self, for Bradley, is identified with that center in ourselves which represents an expanding harmonious individuality. The bad self is identified as the elements within us which cause discord. The Kantian, as we saw, would have to identify the good self with the good will and the bad self with irrational desire. But this did not hold up against the facts of moral experience. That experience recognized the necessity of diminished responsibility which was excluded by Kantian theory. It also recognized that evil had social, as well as individual, roots. Utilitarianism, on the other hand, had argued that the good self was the unselfish self and the bad self the selfish self. But this again runs counter to moral experience. Selfishness is one of the sources of evil, but it is not the only source. Nor is the unselfish person the only source of human good. The unselfish person can still do harm to both himself and others. The bad self is not the selfish self. In fact to use the words "self" or "ego" to refer to the elements of chaos within us is a mistake. The bad self can never give structure to a personality. Its only goal is to disrupt the structure and harmony which the good self creates: "The content of the bad self has no principle, and forms no system, and is relative to no end."[42] Chaos has no principle. Discord is parasitic on harmony, evil on good. For Bradley the existence of goodness is a necessary condition of the existence of evil, but the existence of evil is not a necessary condition for the existence of goodness. We can discover cases of pure benevolence but pure malevolence or cruelty for the sake of cruelty does not exist:

> Our positive self-realization, whether normal or morbid, is still the end of our being. The devil that but denies, the

malevolence that is pure, is no mere ethical monster. It is monstrous too psychologically, and despite Professor Bain's warnings, we must take heart to say that it is not possible.[43]

Man may have a natural capacity for pure benevolence but he has no natural capacity for pure malevolence. "Psychological egoism" has been frequently criticized because it entails the denial of pure malevolence. But as Hobbes noticed, it also implies the denial of pure malevolence:

> For that any man should take pleasure in other men's great harms, without other end of his own, I do not conceive it possible.[44]

If man is not naturally benevolent he is not naturally malevolent either. He could certainly be cruel to others, but only if it furthered his own self-interest. He could never be cruel if he received no pleasure from it. Bradley thought it would be unrealistic to deny the existence of cruelty:

> . . . . Is there real malevolence? That exists and is a clear and palpable fact. It is impossible to deny that cruelty can give pleasure even when there is no ulterior object and aim.[45]

But if real cruelty exists, doesn't this refute psychological egoism? Bain in an attempt to answer the criticism took the unusual defense of admitting the existence of pure cruelty but thought its existence could be explained by his association psychology. Bradley appears to agree with Bain, yet denies that pure malevolence is possible. In doing so he appears to be assimilating "self-realization" to "egoism." He admits that some instances of cruelty can be explained by envy, jealousy or revenge. He also admits that other acts of cruelty might be explained by the pleasure we derive from violence. But his agreement with the utilitarians is superficial. The true explanation of wanton cruelty is the affirmation of strength we receive when we gain power over others:

> There is a desire in human nature to widen the sphere which it can regard as being the expression of its will. And this desire has no boundary. Now the mere existence of another man's will, which is independent of ours, is a limit to this desire, and in consequence we aim at the removal or diminution of that check to our sovereignty. How do we remove the limit? The limit is removed by the subjugation of the other. We must make him a material for our self-assertion, in other words, we must work our will on him.[46]

How are we to do this? We can't achieve it simply by getting him to do what we want, for his submission to our will may be his way of preserving his independence. We have him truly under our will only when we make him do what he most dislikes:

> In this devilish extreme of wanton cruelty
> we have, I presume, got as far as male-
> volence. We do desire the other's pain,
> because only by his pain can we make an
> utter sport and plaything of his will.
> But even here we do not desire his pain
> simply and as such. Even here there is a
> positive ground for our cruelty, and our
> malevolence is never and could never be
> pure.[47]

Bradley is surely right in suggesting that wanton cruelty is an aberration of will rather than desire. Cruel people do not want the pain of others for its own sake, they want absolute power over others. The utilitarian psychologists cannot explain wanton cruelty, because they argue that will is the child of desire. But if wanton cruelty is the child of will, not desire, it can be explained by the self-affirmation we receive when we gain complete power over others, when we enslave them. However this is will gone wrong, for we cannot grow in our relationships with others if we try to destroy their freedom. For Bradley interpersonal relationships call for a higher level of personal growth, one which contains, rather than negates, the moral freedom of those we relate to. For the utilitarian goodness is pleasure and evil is pain. For Bradley pleasure could not be identified with the good, nevertheless he does hold that pleasure is good, and the good is pleasant.

> . . . we must not admit that the pleasant
> as such, is good. The good is pleasant,
> and the better, also; is in proportion
> more pleasant. And we may add, again that

the pleasant is generally good, if we
leave out the 'as such.'[48]

Pleasure is part of the good but it is not good-by-
itself. Bradley also recognizes that pain is an evil.
He says: "No one of course can deny that pain actually
exists, and I at least should not dream of denying that
it is evil."[49] Pain however is not absolutely bad, as
the utilitarians argue, because it can protect us from
harm, and move us towards the good. The essence of pain
is, as we saw, discord, and discord is an essential part
of the more complex psychological phenomena of desire,
will, and self-development. So pain's goodness or
badness must be interpreted in the light of these phenomena and not independent of them, as if it existed in
complete ontological isolation. Pain is also not the
sole evil. There are at least two other kinds of evil,
the frustration which accompanies unrealized goals and
moral evil, the product of the bad self, whose sole
purpose is to undermine the development of the good
self.[50] Frustration is a form of mental pain and it,
like physical pain, is also a form of discord. But the
end of the bad self is to produce discord, to retard and
inhibit the healthy growth of the good self, hence all
three forms of evil have discord as part of their nature.
For Bradley discord is the essence of evil, and discord
also provides the tension which fuels the dynamics of
moral growth. Evil then is a necessary condition for the
existence of morality, but not for the existence of
goodness:

In our moral experience we find this whole
fact given beyond question. We suffer
within ourselves a contest of the good and

the bad wills and a certainty of evil.
Nay, if we please, we may add that this
dischord is necessary, since without it
morality must wholly perish.[51]

Without evil there would be no morality, because
morality is the process of trying to achieve perfect
virtue. Bradley says: "goodness is the realization by
an individual of his own perfection and that perfection
consists in harmony and extent."[52] The essence of
morality is process. We do not spring from our mother's
wombs as full grown moral agents. We go through a
process in becoming the persons we are. The will for
Bradley is neither the slave of the passions, as the
utilitarians believe, nor their master as the Kantian's
believe, for it has its own agenda, the development of
the morally good person.

The theory of virtue which emerges from idealist
psychology is radically different from utilitarian and
Kantian theories. The utilitarian defines virtue as a
trait of character which benefits the self (personal
virtue) or others (moral or social virtue) and vice as a
trait of character which harms the self (personal vice)
or others (moral or social vice).[53] Prudence is an
example of a utilitarian personal virtue; imprudence of a
utilitarian personal vice. Prudence tends to produce
happiness and imprudence unhappiness. Benevolence is an
example of a utilitarian moral or social virtue; malevolence of a utilitarian moral and social vice. Benevolence tends to promote the general happiness and
malevolence the general unhappiness. For the utilitarian
virtue is a means to happiness. It has no intrinsic
value, only instrumental value. A virtue in one context
might be a vice in another context. Benevolence, for

example, could be a virtue in co-operative societies because it would be conducive to the agent's happiness. But in competitive societies it could be a vice because it would be conducive to the agent's misery. For the utilitarian all moral virtue is essentially social.

The Kantian defines virtue as a trait of character which facilitates the conduct of a moral agent (personal or moral virtue) and relationships between moral agents (social virtue). Vice, as a trait of character which inhibits the conduct of a moral agent (personal or moral virtue) and relationships between moral agents (social vice).[54] Courage is an example of a Kantian personal or moral virtue; cowardice an example of a Kantian personal or moral vice. We need courage to act morally in the face of strong fears. Justice is an example of a Kantian social virtue; injustice an example of a Kantian social vice. We need to control our selfish desires in order to be impartial towards other moral agents, to treat them as persons who possess intrinsic value, to act on the principle of respect for persons. For the Kantian virtue is an end-in-itself. The conscientious person does his/her duty because it is the right thing to do and not for rewards or to avoid punishment, and he/she alone possesses intrinsic value. The conscientious person needs to have his/her desires under control if he/she is to act in accordance with rational principles. For the Kantian all moral virtue depends on personal virtue:

> Suppose there were no such duties (duties to the self). There would be no duties at all, not even external ones. For I cannot recognize myself as bound to others except in so far as I bind myself at the same time. . . .[55]

The idealist defines a virtue as a personality structure which facilitates the moral development of the agent (personal/moral virtue) and the growth of interpersonal and social relationships (social/moral virtue). A vice is a personality structure which retards the moral development of the agent (personal/moral vice) and the growth of interpersonal and social relationships (social/moral vice). For the idealist moral virtue is simultaneously personal and interpersonal. Courage is certainly a personal virtue for the idealist. We need courage in order to grow morally. But it is also a social virtue. A society permeated with courage will be able to carry out policies which are compatible with the individual moral development of its members. Benevolence is certainly a social virtue. We need to care for others if a society is to organize its institutions in a way which will support, rather than retard, the individual moral development of its members. But it is also a personal virtue. Self love is as important as love of others for moral growth. They are mutually dependent. Someone who does not love himself is not likely to be able to love others. A theory of virtue and vice must account for the fact that we normally consider both personal and social virtues to be distinct yet moral virtues. Kantianism accounts for personal moral virtue but not social moral virtue. Utilitarianism accounts for social moral virtue but not personal moral virtue. Bradley's idealism can account for both, hence it proves itself to be more complete and hence the better theory. It is both more integrated and more comprehensive.

The idealist theory of virtue differs from the utilitarian and Kantian theories in even more significant ways. For the utilitarian will is the slave of the passions; for Kant it is their master. For the idealist it is neither of these. Rather the will is the conscious core of the growing person, one that is trying always to become richer and more harmonious: "The end I take to be the fullest and most harmonious development of our being."[56] To reach it we all go through a process of development. To understand it we need to examine in some detail how morality evolves in the individual moral agent.

NOTES

Chapter IV: Self-Realization and Egoism

1   F. H. Bradley, Ethical Studies, p. 65.
2   F. H. Bradley, Ibid., p. 66.
3   F. H. Bradley, Ibid., p. 66. Cf. my The Moral Question: Ethical Theory, Chapter 2.
4   F. H. Bradley, Ibid., p. 67.
5   F. H. Bradley, Ibid., pp. 252-253.
6   F. H. Bradley, Ibid., p. 254.
7   Cf. Chapter II, pp. 43-55.
8   F. H. Bradley, Ethical Studies, p. 252.
9   J. S. Mill, "Utilitarianism," Collected Works (Volume X), pp. 227-233.
10   Kant, Ethical Philosophy, "The Metaphysics of Morals," p. 59.
11   J. S. Mill, "Utilitarianism," The Collected Works, pp. 227-233.
12   J. S. Mill, Ibid., p. 230.
13   J. S. Mill, Ibid., pp. 235-237.
14   J. S. Mill, "Utilitarianism," pp. 234-235.
15   J. S. Mill, "Utilitarianism," p. 236.
16   J. S. Mill, Ibid., p. 231, and James Mill, Analysis of The Phenomena of the Human Mind, p. 286.
17   F. H. Bradley, "Sympathy and Interest," Collected Essays, p. 138.
18   F. H. Bradley, Ibid., p. 138.
19   F. H. Bradley, Ibid., p. 138.
20   F. H. Bradley, Ibid., p. 139.
21   F. H. Bradley, Ibid., p. 141.
22   F. H. Bradley, Ethical Studies, pp. 67-68.
23   F. H. Bradley, Ibid., p. 68.

24 F. H. Bradley, "Association and Thought," Collected Essays, p. 212.
25 F. H. Bradley, Ibid., pp. 230-231.
26 F. H. Bradley, Ibid., p. 210.
27 F. H. Bradley, Ibid., p. 211.
28 F. H. Bradley, "Coherence and Contradiction," Essays on Truth and Reality, p. 223.
29 F. H. Bradley, Ibid., p. 223 and Ethical Studies, p. 74 (footnote 1).
30 F. H. Bradley, "Association and Thought," Collected Essays, p. 231 (footnote 1).
31 F. H. Bradley, "On Pleasure, Pain, Desire and Volition," Collected Essays, pp. 244-248.
32 F. H. Bradley, Ibid., p. 248.
33 F. H. Bradley, Ibid., p. 248.
34 F. H. Bradley, Ibid., p. 251.
35 F. H. Bradley, Ibid., p. 260.
36 F. H. Bradley, Ibid., p. 263. The same position is developed, although less clearly, in Ethical Studies, pp. 262-274.
37 F. H. Bradley, Ibid., p. 272.
38 F. H. Bradley, Ibid., p. 272.
39 F. H. Bradley, "The Definition of Will (1)," Collected Essays, pp. 502-503. Bradley's position on the relation of will and desire was less clearly developed in Ethical Studies, but the account given there in chapters 3 and 7 implicitly contains the later positions of the Essays. Cf. Ethical Studies, pp. 73-74.
40 F. H. Bradley, "On Pleasure, Pain, Desire and Volition," p. 283.
41 F. H. Bradley, Ethical Studies, pp. 276-277.
42 F. H. Bradley, Ibid., p. 280.

43 F. H. Bradley, "Is there such a thing as Pure Malevolence?," Collected Essays, p. 137.

44 Thomas Hobbes, Leviathan (Book I), Liberal Arts, 1958, p. 58.

45 F. H. Bradley, "Is there such a thing as Pure Malevolence?," p. 133.

46 F. H. Bradley, Ibid., pp. 135-136.

47 F. H. Bradley, Ibid., p. 136.

48 F. H. Bradley, Appearance and Reality, pp. 357-358.

49 F. H. Bradley, Ibid., pp. 174-175.

50 F. H. Bradley, Ibid., p. 174.

51 F. H. Bradley, Ibid., p. 178.

52 F. H. Bradley, Ibid., p. 367; cf. Ethical Studies, p. 74.

53 D. Hume, An enquiry concerning the Principles of Morals, Liberal Arts, 1957.

54 Kant, Ethical Philosophy (The Metaphysics of Morals), p. 77ff.

55 Kant, Ibid., p. 78.

56 F. H. Bradley, Essays on Truth and Reality, p. 86.

CHAPTER V
The Stages of the Moral Life

In chapters 5, 6, 7, and in the "Concluding Remarks" of Ethical Studies, Bradley develops a theory of ethics, which is designed to make good the inadequacies of utilitarianism and Kantianism.[1] A central concept in that theory is that of "My Station and Its Duties." Since we are all members of communities we all have social roles to play. Our duties, rights, privileges and freedoms are defined by the stations we occupy in life. We are citizens, teachers, students, fathers, mothers, husbands, wives, sons, daughters, brothers, sisters, doctors, dentists, lawyers, ministers, priests, Christians, Jews, Muslims, men and women. To be moral is to act in accordance with the rules imposed on us by the social groups to which we belong. It is by living in terms of our social roles that we are able to realize ourselves, to develop harmonious personalities. The end for man can be redefined as "his function as an organ in a social organism."[2] This theory can be called "ethical institutionalism," i.e., the rightness or wrongness of an action is determined by the social institutions we belong to.

Bradley has been strongly criticized for holding what appears to be a radical form of "ethical conformism," i.e., the view that the rightness or wrongness of an action is determined by the rules in practise in a particular society. There is no doubt that the concept of "my station and its duties" is pivotal in Bradley's ethical theory, but he always denied that this was all there was to it. The theory is not complete until it is integrated with the "ideal morality" of chapter 6, and the developmental psychology worked out in chapter 7, and

"The Concluding Remarks," of Ethical Studies. Some of Bradley's critics are aware of his claim, but insist that the institutionalism of chapter 5 completely contradicts the individualism of chapter 6 and denies individual freedom. Henry Sidgwick, in a famous review of Ethical Studies, argued that no matter how Bradley tries to modify the concept of "My Station and its Duties," in the end he cannot escape the basic thesis that right conduct means conformity to an existing moral code which is relative to time and place.[3] Ethical institutionalism also implies ethical relativism. Relativism maintains that the rightness or wrongness of an action is determined by the emotive or cognitive attitude a society has towards it. On this theory no real moral disagreement can occur between different societies. For example Canada feels that racism is immoral but South Africa feels it is morally acceptable, yet we really do not disagree. There is no contradiction for we are merely expressing our society's moral preferences and they theirs. There is no rational way of deciding between them. We cannot argue that our attitudes are morally better than theirs. They are just different. For relativism the moral values of every culture are equally valid. Bradley's idealism then cannot provide any objective method for determining what is right and wrong. Hence it is less successful as an ethical theory than Utilitarianism or Kantianism which both provide objective standards of right and wrong: Utilitarianism, the principle of utility; and Kantianism, the principle of respect for persons. Sidgwick's criticisms cannot be properly addressed until Bradley's developmental psychology has been examined.

Bradley agrees with the utilitarians that conscience is acquired, rather than innate, as Kant and other rationalists believed. He agrees that morality is a process:

> We do not begin with a consciousness of
> good and evil, right and wrong, as such,
> or in a strict sense. The child is taught
> to will a content which is universal and
> good, and he learns to identify his will
> with it, so that he feels pleasure when he
> feels himself in accord with it, uneasi-
> ness and pain when his will is contrary
> thereto, and he <u>feels</u> that it is con-
> trary.[4]

Although Bradley agrees with the utilitarians that conscience is acquired, he disagrees with the function they assign to conscience, and the way they describe and explain its development. In order to explain how we acquire the capacity to think and act in accordance with universal moral principles a different theory of moral development is required.[5] For Bradley moral development evolves through a sequence of distinct stages:

> This realization is possible only by the
> individual's living as a member in a
> higher life, and this higher life is
> slowly developed in a series of stages.[6]

Each stage is characterized by a distinct mode of thinking about the world and of responding emotionally to it. These different aspects of our experience are organically related. As Bradley says: "It is better to treat the mind as a single phenomenon, progressing through stages. . . ."[7] Each higher stage represents a more morally adequate way of relating to the world than the previous stage. Moral development is governed by the law of individuation. We have a basic drive to structure our experience, to make it as rich and integrated as possible. The process is continuous, hence dividing it into stages is, to some extent, arbitrary, and false. The stage theory is a hypothesis which Bradley thinks will help us to comprehend our moral experience. It doesn't matter then if it partially misrepresents our experience, so long as it helps us to understand it. There are at least four stages; Stage One: Egotistical Hedonism, Stage Two: Institutionalism, Stage Three: Personalism, Stage Four: Metaphysical Mysticism.[8]

Stage One: Egotistical Hedonism

In the beginning the child's experience is an undifferentiated unity:

> In the beginning there is nothing beyond
> what is presented, what is and is felt, or
> rather is felt simply. There is no memory
> or imagination or hope or fear or thought
> or will, and no perception of differences
> or likeness. There are, in short, no
> relations and no feelings, only feeling.[9]

The child makes no distinction between itself and objects outside itself. Self-awareness and awareness of objects develops simultaneously. The child interacting pleasantly and painfully with the environment produces a sense of self-awareness: "What we start with in the child is the feeling of himself affirmed or negated in this or that situation."[10] The sense of self first develops through sensation. For example, the child touches itself and feels itself touching other things, and being touched by others. And all these experiences have a single reference, the self.[11] Self-awareness develops further through the active interest the child now takes in its surroundings. These feelings are objectified in things, in impermanent objects, which satisfy the child's simple appetites for food and warmth, etc.

Stage one is essentially an egocentric or narcissistic stage. The child is primarily concerned with the immediate consequences of his behaviour which produces pleasure and pain for the self. If it possessed a morality at all it could be described as proto-utilitarian, because in it the child is essentially concerned with the hedonistic consequences of particular actions. Whether conscience proper can be said to exist at this stage is questionable. Nevertheless, a rudimentary form of conscience does appear. As self-awareness develops, so does the capacity of the child to become dissatisfied with itself, for not successfully getting pleasure. The moral emotions of guilt and shame, associated with loss of self-esteem, have appeared on the scene in rudimentary form.[12]

Thought, like morality, begins to develop out of undifferentiated experience in stage one. At the earliest point in its history, the primitive mind does not make explicit judgements:

> It cannot judge, for it has no ideas. It
> cannot distinguish its images from fact,
> and so it cannot unite them consciously to
> the world of reality. And thus it cannot

reason; for it inference, if it had one,
would end in fact, not in a truth.[13]

Although the lowest stages of mind are confined to
the apprehension of simple sensations, it is a mistake,
Bradley suggests, to think that it is purely passive:

> For in the very lowest stage of psychical
> existence we can still point to a central
> activity, and verify there a rudiment of
> inference. And a soul, so far as we are
> able to see, would be no soul at all if it
> had not this centre.[14]

Even in its earliest manifestations the mind is an
active center, which is already interpreting experience
through ideas, though it is unaware it is doing so.
Bradley thinks it's best to assume that the law of
individuation is at work in the earliest as well as the
later stages of mental development. The process is a
continuum from infancy to adulthood. Significant developments however do occur which mark off one stage from
another:

> Thus with judgement we are sure that, at a
> certain stage, it does not exist, and at a
> latter stage it is found in operation.[15]

There is, however, no sharp break between stages.
One shades into another. This is why Bradley believes
that a single unifying hypothesis is required to explain
both moral and cognitive development. We must assume
that even the earliest stages of mental development
operate under the organic law of individuation. This is

why association psychology cannot account for the development of moral agency or higher cognitive activity. If stage one were organized on the mechanical principles postulated by the utilitarians, and contained only individual impressions, then stage two, which makes use of universal symbols, would never occur. If what you have in stage one is particular impressions grouped by the mechanical laws of association, then judgement and the search for truth would never arise:

> But the fashionable doctrine of association, in which images are recalled by and unite with particular images, is, I think, not true of any stage of mind. [16]

Just as there is no sharp distinction between the stages of cognitive or moral development, so, for Bradley, there is no sharp distinction between human and animal intelligence. Animals reason and judge in the same primitive sense, as humans do in stage one:

> And thus, in a sense, the lowest animals both judge and reason, and unless they did so, they must cease to adjust their actions to the environment. But in a strict sense, they can neither reason nor judge, for they do not distinguish between ideas and perceived reality. [17]

Animals may not consciously use ideas as symbols, but activities like the stalking of prey, indicate the presence of intentional behaviour of the kind associated with unsatisfied desire. The same behaviour, Bradley thinks, suggests that a primitive form of morality exists in animals as it does for humans in stage one:

> The dissatisfied brooding of an animal that has, for example, missed its prey, is, we may be sure, not yet moral. But it will none the less contain in rudiment that judgement of one self which is a most important factor in morality.[18]

Animals must be credited with intelligence and emotions which function by the same principles as human intelligence and emotions. Nor does the fact of human language alter this interpretation. Bradley thinks that pre-linguistic thought exists and so language is not a necessary condition of judgement and reasoning:

> . . . in the stage before language, there are mental phenomena which certainly suggest the effective distinction of sensation and idea.[19]

Language does develop in stage one, and although it is not essential to the development of judgement, it does facilitate the process. It might appear that Bradley is guilty here of anthropomorphism, of reading into animal behaviour human qualities which are not there. Bradley's views could be dismissed as an expression of Victorian sentimentalism towards animals. Association psychology may be inappropriate when applied to the behaviour of human infants but it can explain animal behaviour. Bradley is not sentimentalizing animals. He is putting forward the hypothesis that we can explain animal behaviour better if we use organic principles, like the

law of individuation, than if we use mechanical principles, like the laws of association developed by stimulus-
response psychologists. Bradley's hypothesis is surely
worth taking seriously because it is normally adopted in
our dealings with animals. A farmer knows that his pigs
have feelings, needs, intelligence, form intentions, and
have minds of their own, because these assumptions
facilitate his/her interaction with them. The hypothesis
is true because it works at the practical level. It
could also work at the theoretical level. The analogy
between animal and human intelligence is important in
other ways. Bradley believes that animal and stage one
human intelligence are completely dominated by the
practical:

> For the early soul-life (it is a truth we
> can not repeat too often) is immersed in
> practise. It is wholly directed to the
> satisfaction of its appetite, first for
> food, and then for the continuance of its
> species.[20]

Stage one is the stage of practical or instrumental
intelligence, of the adaption of means to immediate ends.
The basic learning process is one of trial and error
which proceeds by simple generalization from experience.
True universals which form the basis of theoretical
judgement, and hypothesis formation, are not yet in use.
Animals and infants may have practical curiosity but they
do not have fully developed theoretical curiosity.[21] In
stage one self-interest rules and reason is the slave of
passion.

In stage one the virtues would possess only instrumental value. They would have no intrinsic value. The

characteristic virtue, although only rudimentally developed, would be prudence. The characteristic vice would be selfishness. This stage also provides the prototype of the voluptuary. The true voluptuary does not emerge until the pursuit of pleasure becomes a conscious and permanent way of life:

> The voluptuary, was not always what he is. Children are supposed to pursue the pleasant, but no one ever calls a young child a voluptuary, and everybody has been a child. Our voluptuary at first, that is, when his consciousness had arrived at a stage where objects existed for him, and he began to desire them, pursued chance pleasant things without reflection. And to this stage of desire for this or that pleasant thing we may give the name 'appetite.'[22]

The individual is at the center of the moral universe and takes no heed of social morality. Indeed, at this stage, the child does not yet understand the idea of a morality which exists beyond the self. Towards the end of this stage, greater self-awareness is achieved through the child's interaction and identification with his/her parents, especially the mother, on whom the child depends to fulfill his/her needs. His/her pleasure and pain now become bound up with the pleasure and pain of the persons who nurture him/her. If they are happy, he/she is happy. If they are unhappy, he/she is unhappy. The dichotomy between the self and others ceases to exist towards the end of this stage and moral education proper starts:

> At this point we have reached the stage
> when moral education begins; not that the
> child will be a moral being as yet; but it
> is here that we can see the unconscious
> beginnings of a better and a worse self.[23]

The child also becomes more complex emotionally.
His/her interests begin to attach themselves to objects
which are relatively permanent:

> Mother and nurse satisfy a child's recur-
> ring wants; but they are pleasant to him
> in other respects, and are always with
> him, so that he feels them as part of
> himself, and when left alone is uneasy and
> wants them.[24]

Permanent desire has replaced simple appetite as the
predominant form of feeling in the child. This provides
the child with the emotional stability and security which
facilitates growth to a higher stage of development. The
voluptuary or the psychopath, who has no concern for
others, need not appear.

Significant cognitive development also occurs
towards the end of stage one. In the lowest stages of
mind there is a primitive awareness of the distinction
between data and its interpretation. But since intelligence here is primarily practical and instrumental, no
distinction is drawn between sensation and idea. The
image is not used symbolically so it is not a true idea.
The distinction between appearance and reality has not
yet emerged:

> That the thing as it is, and as it appears
> in perception are not the same thing, is,
> we all are aware, a very late after-
> thought. But it is equally an after-
> thought, though not equally late, that
> there is any kind of difference between
> ideas and impressions.[25]

In stage one the child develops the capacity to use
symbolic, universal, abstract ideas, and this helps the
development of theoretical reasoning. It is the experience of error which generates the distinction between
appearance and reality, and with this basic metaphysical
notion we have the true beginning of the theoretical
mind:

> The fact of illusion and error is in
> various ways forced early upon the mind,
> and the ideas by which we try to under-
> stand the universe, may be considered as
> attempts to set right our failure.[26]

Without the distinction between appearance and
reality, and the experience of contradiction, the search
for truth, as a distinct function of the mind, would
never arise. It is this development which separates
humans from animals. Bradley doesn't think animals
develop past the stage of instrumental intelligence.
They have no pure theoretical curiosity. They may
encounter illusion and error in their experience but it
has no theoretical significance for them:

> And, if we descend in the scale no further
> than dogs, we are struck by the absence of

theoretical curiosity. Let them see an
appearance to be not what is seemed, and
it instantly becomes a mere nonentity.[27]

The dog, like the child in stage one, is immersed in
the practical and what interests it is determined by
immediate want. If the dog had a metaphysic, if it
distinguished between appearance and reality, it would be
rooted in practise. As Bradley said, if a dog had a
logic its basic axiom would be: "What is smells, and
what does not smell is nothing."[28] Because of its
capacity for symbolic thought, the human child relates to
error in a different way than the higher animals. For it
is in response to frustrated desire that the child begins
to develop theoretical reasoning:

> And the pain of accident or unsatisfied
> desire will force the soul to consider
> this contrast, and to make explicit the
> difference it must feel. Both in theory
> and in history, it is mishap and defect on
> the practical side which gives birth to
> speculation.[29]

With the development of the theoretical mind, the
way has been paved for growth to a higher stage of moral
development.

Stage Two: Institutionalism

In this stage the child begins to act in accordance
with the rules of the social groups to which he belongs;
the family, peer groups, the churches, the schools, and

the nation. Although morality existed in a rudimentary
form is stage one, it is in stage two that moral education begins and the true moral agent appears. The moral
agent first develops through the interaction of the
child's developing will with the will of others. The
child discovers himself/herself to be limited and controlled by those he/she loves, those he/she has identified with. The pleasure and pain of the mother is now
related to the child's desires and conduct, as well as
his/her appetites. What he/she does either pleases or
pains the mother, and so pleases or pains the child.
When his/her mother is unhappy with his/her conduct,
he/she is unhappy with himself/herself and the way he/she
behaves. When his/her mother is happy with his/her
conduct, he/she is happy with himself/herself and the way
he/she behaves:

> The pleasure or pain of the mother and the
> nurse has been his pleasure or pain, and
> now he learns by experience that this
> pleasure and pain are related to certain
> things which he does or leaves undone. He
> sees what displeasure means, and what it
> is when others are pleased with him. He
> learns that the external, with which he is
> identified, is a will which can be assert-
> ed against himself with painful conse-
> quences, and that these pleasant or
> painful assertions in relation to himself
> are connected with certain classes of his
> own activities.[30]

Conformity to the will of others means he is in
harmony with his world. Non-conformity means discord and

unhappiness. At this point harmony, happiness, and good conduct become structurally bound up with each other and discord, distress, and bad conduct become similarly united. The moral emotions of guilt and shame are now dependent on the way others see us. Our self-image and self-esteem are in the hands of others. We are proud of ourselves when those who matter to us are proud of us. We are ashamed of ourselves when they are ashamed of us. In stage two the child becomes moralized. It learns to follow moral rules which are perceived as external, universal (apply to classes of acts), and binding (obligatory). He/she begins to act on rules and principles, to order his/her life by universal prescriptions. The principle of universalizability now controls moral reasoning. The process of moralization is gradual and not fully reflective:

> Not that he reflects much, if at all; he feels pleasure when in accord with a superior, pain when antagonistic, and the particular stages of the process whereby he comes to do so, are not before his mind at all.[31]

Although there is no awareness of the process, the moral agent begins to emerge. The capacity to act in accordance with moral rules and principles develops, along with the capacity to act in purely disinterested and unselfish ways:

> A child, when it tries to please its mother is as unselfish as the hen, who faces death for her chickens, as unselfish

as the dog who gives his life for his master.[32]

The morality of stage two is essentially non-consequentialist. Rightness and wrongness are defined by conformity or non-conformity to moral rules. This stage can be called proto-Kantian, because in it moral rules take epistemological precedence over the actual consequences of actions. Conscientiousness becomes the principle virtue: "To will what the superior wills is an end-in-itself."[33] Disobedience, disloyalty and negligence become the principle vices:

> Obedience to command, pleasing the superior is pleasant and a desired end; disobedience and the superior's displeasure is in itself painful and avoided.[34]

One does one's duty for the sake of duty, and we expect others to do the same. We want to see the traditions of our group manifest in others as well as ourselves. The child becomes a firm supporter of law, social order, and citizen's rights. He/she learns that possessing rights implies accepting obligations. The social virtues of justice and benevolence become ends-in-themselves, and take precedence over the personal virtues in cases of conflict. Self-sacrifice is honored though not required. The perfect duties of justice take precedence over the imperfect duties of beneficence. Rights take precedence over charity.

Stage two cannot be called Kantianism proper, because it is also conventional, conformist and relativistic. To be moral at this stage means to live by the traditions and conventions of the social groups to which we belong, so it also proto-idealistic. Our obligations are defined by our social roles. To be obligated means to have duties imposed on us by others. Failure to be dutiful gives others the right to be displeased with us, and to punish us if necessary. The notion that society has a right to control the conduct of its members becomes central, and morality tends to be equated with the social control of the individual.

In stage two thought becomes symbolic, universal, hypothetical and abstract:

> Our object here has been, in passing, to show that the symbolic use of ideas in judgement, although no early process of the mind, is a natural result of mental development.[35]

A clear distinction is now drawn between sensations and mental images which are particular, and ideas which are symbolic and universal. Truth and falsehood depend, Bradley suggests, on the relations our ideas have to reality. Judgement proper, then, presupposes ideas which are recognized as symbols, as something which has significance beyond its instantiation as a particular mental event. Without symbols there would be no judgement or theoretical reasoning: "Ideas are not ideas until they are symbols, and before we use symbols we cannot judge."[36] The stage has been reached where we consciously need to give order and meaning to our experience. The rudimentary judgements of stage one were categorical and concrete. They dealt directly with reality: "At a low stage of mind where everything is fact . . . it (hypothetical judgement) could not exist."[37] The judgements of stage two are hypothetical and abstract. They deal directly with reality through symbolic ideas. Hypothesis formation and testing through ideal experiment become the dominant mode of thought. Theoretical and scientific reasoning now appear.

In stage two thought frees itself from the bondage of the passions and begins to pursue its own agenda. The pursuit of truth has become an end-in-itself. It possesses intrinsic, and not merely instrumental, value:

> . . . what is certain is this, that at the beginning of progress the intellect is subordinate, and that afterwards it becomes at least partially free.[38]

Stage two represents an advance over stage one because it is better developed intellectually, emotionally and morally. Thought is richer and more sophisticated. The function of hypotheses and universal judgements, in both theoretical and practical reasoning, is understood. Moral thinking makes use of universal principles, and no longer relies on simple generalizations from experience. The function of moral rules and systems of rules in social organizations is accepted and acted on. The idea that moral rules apply to all members of a social group and not just the self becomes the prevailing attitude. The child is capable of applying the principle of universalizability in the context of the groups he/she belongs to. He/she understands that what is a good, or a right, or a liberty, for one member of the group, is a good or a right or a liberty for any other member of the group. The child's moral universe expands to include the family, friends, peers and countrymen.

Emotionally stage two is also more developed than stage one. For one thing, desire has replaced appetite as the basic emotional structure of the child. Satisfaction of desire is now the prime goal of the child. But desires are complex and involve the need for harmony and growth. The child wants harmony in its emotions, its thought and its conduct. For another, the happiness of self and the happiness of others has become structurally bound up, so the moral consciousness has expanded emotionally, as well as intellectually, to include others. The content of the individual's conscience is the same as that of the main social groups to which he/she belongs. At this stage personal and social morality are integrated. A true moral agent is present and functioning.

Stage two is, however, not the final stage in the development of the moral agent. To be fully moral, the agent must be aware that he/she is a moral being. He/she must take charge of his/her morality, and this does not happen until stage three has been reached. The change from stage two to stage three morality can only be understood by examining the development of the bad self:

> But before we pass from unconscious to conscious good, and with that morality, we must trace the growth of the bad self (not known as such) in order to see how knowledge of good and bad arises from their collision in a self-conscious subject.[39]

It is during stage two that the bad self begins to make its appearance. The bad self, as we saw, is an unsystematic set of pursuits which continually collides with the good. The purpose of the bad self, if it can be said to have one, is to disrupt the structure and harmony

which the good self produces. The bad self emerges now
because conscience is the product of a contest of wills.
The child begins to get pleasure from doing things which
his/her parents prohibit, and in not doing things his
parents require. The child delights in rebelling against
moral authority. The bad self is paradoxical because it
can both inhibit and stimulate moral development.
Rebellion can retard growth so that the child remains
permanently trapped at stage one. He/she then becomes
the voluptuary, who turns the natural desire for pleasure
into lust, or the psychopath who has no concern for
others, or the radical individualist who is alienated
from, and hostile to, the society he lives in. In all
these cases the person has failed to mature morally. But
rebellion can also stimulate growth because socialization
is never perfect. In the first place, Bradley points
out, the process of socialization will vary according to
individual circumstances, hence imperfectly socialized
people will be produced, people who find it extremely
difficult to conform to the mores of the community.[40]
And even the fully socialized person does not necessarily
rid himself/herself of the bad self. This can only be
achieved while he/she is performing his/her role as a
member of a community. But no one does this all of the
time. He/she would only be fully moral when he/she is
"on duty" and not necessarily when he/she is "off duty."
More importantly the communities with which the agent
identifies himself/herself may be imperfect:

> It is necessary to remark that the commu-
> nity in which he is a member may be in a
> confused or rotten condition, so that in
> it right and might do not always go
> to-gether.[41]

Finally we are more than our social roles. We need to realize ourselves as more than social beings. As Bradley says: "The making myself better does not always directly involve relations with others."[42] The instability which the bad self introduces into stage two provides the dynamics which impel the moral agent to move to a higher stage of development.

Stage Three: Personalism

In stage three morality becomes self-conscious, critical, and personal:

> In the higher form of volition (so much cannot be disputed) we come upon an important difference. Our will at this stage has become reflective. I do not here identify myself immediately with this or that practical suggestion, but on the contrary I regard these as things offered to me for my acceptance or rejection.[43]

Stage three is the stage of the fully developed moral agent, who consciously assents to rational principles and rules (universal prescriptions), and thinks, and acts in terms of them. He is now a self-legislating moral being. His moral life is now governed by fundamental moral principles, like respect for persons, respect for human life, benevolence, non-malevolence, impartiality, fairness, and self-perfection. The agent tries to be consistent in thought, action, and feeling, and to produce a coherent system of morality. He/she consciously applies the principle of individuation as the standard for this morality. Thought, feeling and conduct will be morally appropriate if they facilitate the development of a richer and more integrated person. They will be morally inappropriate if they retard, inhibit or regress the development of a richer, more integrated person. The morality of stage three is truly universal and no longer relative to the societies in which we live. We begin to develop what Bradley calls a "cosmopolitan morality":

> Men nowadays know to some extent what is thought right and wrong in other communities now, and what has been thought at other times; and this leads to a notion of goodness not of any particular time and country.[44]

The universal morality which emerges here is one which evolves out of the relativistic moralities of stage two. It is not one in which social engineers force a utopia onto a real, growing society:

> The notion that full-fledged moral ideas fall down from heaven is contrary to all the facts with which we are acquainted.[45]

Progress for Bradley, at both the social and personal levels, is evolutionary rather than revolutionary. There is no ideal plan for realizing the morally perfect society, any more than there is one for realizing the morally perfect person. Societies, like persons, have the right to develop autonomously without foreign interferences. There is a sense in which morality will always be relative. Morality exists only in societies and their members. It will always be individuated in particular cultures and persons which are located in particular spaces and times. It shouldn't surprise anyone, then, to discover that morality is in fact diverse in both time and space:

> It is abundantly clear that the morality of one time is not that of another time, that the men considered good in one age might in another age not be thought good, and what would be right for us here might be mean and base in another country, and what would be wrong for us here might there be our bounden duty.[46]

The fact of moral diversity could mislead us into believing that morality is purely conventional, in the sense that the rightness or wrongness of actions is determined by the attitudes a society has towards them.[47] If this were true then moral judgements would simply be expressions of the preference of our society and would have no objective validity. Moral knowledge would be a chimera. Moral skepticism would triumph, and morality would vanish: "If what is right here is wrong there, then all morality (such is the notion) would vanish."[48]

The common error here is to confuse contextualism with subjectivism. To say that the rightness or wrongness of an action depends on the time and place of its occurrence is not to say it is merely a matter of personal or societal preference. What is right for one society may indeed by wrong for another. But this does not mean that these judgements are subjective. If the policy does make it richer and more harmonious as a society then the policy is valid. If it is able to express more values without conflict than it did before then genuine progress has been achieved. If the policy retards, inhibits or regresses the development towards a richer, more harmonious society, it is invalid. The principle of individuation provides a criterion for criticizing both our own or other societies which takes into account the context of national history, but yet is not subjective.

In stage three the ideal moral being is one who is capable of realizing himself/herself in any of the morally imperfect communities in which he/she finds himself/herself. Morality now becomes personal as well as social. We recognize that morality is not confined to social morality. It has a private as well as a public part. There are aspects of our lives which do not belong to the community. Not to develop these aspects would be a failure to realize self.

Stage three represents an advance over stage two because it is better developed intellectually, emotionally and morally. Moral thought is now more sophisticated, systematic and comprehensive. It is both consequentialist and non-consequentialist. It is fully conscious of the dialectical relations which hold between rules and their particular instantiations. Rules do not automatically take precedence over particular judgements, and vice versa. It gives the same weight to consequentialist principles as it does to non-consequentialist principles. Duties of justice do not automatically take precedence over duties of beneficence, and vice versa. Conflicts of duties are resolved by appeal to the principle of individuation. If a course of action facilitates the moral development of the agent it is valid, if it retards, inhibits or regresses that development, it is invalid. At this level moral judgement is concrete and pays attention to the nuances of context.

In stage three critical moral reflection has replaced uncritical acceptance of conventional standards.

To be obligated means to act in accordance with right
reason rather than obey the moral dictates of others.
The moral explorer, who must sail unchartered and often
perilous seas, is born. Moral thought has become truly
universal and is no longer subjective or relativistic.
Moral judgements do not depend on the attitude (emotive
or cognitive) of any person or group of persons, as they
did in stages one and two. The rightness or wrongness of
actions is now determined by the objective standards of
richness and integration, which are valid for all rational beings. Morality now embraces the whole of humanity
and not just the social groups to which the moral agent
belongs.

Stage three is also emotionally richer than stages
one and two. It takes into account the personal as well
as the social side of morality, and recognizes the
inadequacies of conventionalism. If the moral agent does
not move to this stage he will remain permanently trapped
in stage two, unable to escape the restrictions of his
conventional morality. He will never become a mature
moral agent, an autonomous seeker of virtue. His morality will become rule-bound, rigid, and oppressive. He
will no longer be able to learn and grow from experience.
However great an improvement stage three is over stage
two, it still remains imperfect, and its dynamics point
toward a fourth and still higher stage:

> Morality is an endless process, and
> therefore a self-contradiction; and, being
> such, it does not remain standing in
> itself, but feels the impulse to transcend
> its existing reality. [49]

Morality is a process, and all processes are by nature self-contradictory:

> Evolution is a contradiction; and, when the contradiction ceases, the evolution ceases. The process is a contradiction, and only because it is a contradiction can it be a process.[50]

It is the discordant elements of contradiction and pain which drive the psyche to higher levels of existence. This is why moral dilemmas play a central role in the dynamics of moral growth. Morality is ultimately self-contradictory because it demands what cannot be, that everyone be perfect, and this is impossible. So long as mankind is what it is, this will never happen. Morality, since it always will be imperfectly realized in ourselves and the world, implies that it must move beyond itself to a level of consciousness where it is transformed into another form of existence, like the caterpillar into the butterfly. In this fourth stage, morality fuses with religion, metaphysics and mysticism:

> Reflection on morality leads us beyond it. It leads, in short, to see the necessity of a religious point of view. It certainly does not tell us that morality comes first in the world and then religion: what it tells us is that morality is imperfect, and imperfect in such a way as implies a higher, which is religion.[51]

Stage Four: Metaphysical Mysticism

In this stage morality, properly speaking, ceases to exist. In it we go beyond good and evil as seen from the moral perspective. Since evil helps to fuel the moral process, evil is a necessary aspect of morality, something which cannot be eliminated until morality itself has ceased to be:

> For morality desires unconsciously, with the suppression of evil, to become wholly non-moral. . . . Morality itself, which makes evil, desires in evil to remove a condition of its own being. It labours essentially to pass into a super-moral and therefore a non-moral sphere.[52]

The existence of pain, suffering, frustrated desire, and immorality (the harm we do ourselves and others), raises the question of whether morality itself is good or bad. This question cannot be understood from within morality, so we are forced to go beyond it to find answers. Religion is where Bradley suggests we look to discover a different and more inclusive perspective of good and evil. Bradley is not suggesting we base our ethics on religion, but to recognize that religion and ethics intermix in our ordinary moral experience. We cannot base ethics on religion because morality is one of the criteria we use to evaluate religion:

> That there is some connection between true religion and morality everyone we need consider sees. A man who is 'religious'

and does not act morally, is an imposter, or his religion is a false one.[53]

Religion is of course more than morality. It involves, according to Bradley, a belief in, and a devotion to, a perfect being who is utterly good.[54] For religion the ideal actually exists; for morality it is something to strive for. To be moral at this stage means to act in accordance with the dictates of the Divine will. And this involves the subjection of the personal will to the Divine will:

> You must resolve to give up your will, as the mere will of this or that man, and you must put your whole self, your entire will, into the will of the divine.[55]

Stage four, like stage two, requires the subordination of the agent's will to an external will. But at this stage the will the agent identifies with is morally perfect and real. In Ethical Studies, Bradley held that the content of ethics does not change at the religious level: ". . . the content of religion and morality is the same, though the spirit in which it is done is widely different."[56] The religious consciousness, for Bradley, is a general way of viewing and responding emotionally to the universe as a whole: "It is the belief 'with the heart' that is wanted; and where that is not, religion is not."[57] Religion is not to be identified with its external trappings, like accepting creeds, attending church and saying prayers:

> The true doctrine is that devotional exercises and sacraments, and church

goings, not only should not and ought not
go by themselves, but that by themselves
are not religious at all.[58]

The religious consciousness is a mystical attitude
towards creation which can exist without sacraments or
public worship.[59]   Stage four is essentially a development of personal rather than social morality.

In Appearance and Reality, Bradley seems to suggest
that mysticism is not merely an attitude towards morality, but that it has a special content as well. For the
religious consciousness everything which exists is good:

> For religion all is the perfect expression
> of a supreme will, and all things are
> therefore good. Everything is perfect and
> evil, the conscious bad will itself, is
> taken up into and subserves this absolute
> end.[60]

The fundamental moral attitude of the religious
consciousness is the sanctity of existence, i.e., existence is better than non-existence. A universe in which
evil exists is better than no universe at all:

> . . . how am I to know that pain, crime,
> and self-sacrifice are really undesirable?
> I do not see how to affirm this, unless I
> am prepared to say that the world as it
> stands is worse than nothing. . . .[61]

For the mystic all existence possesses value. The
whole of nature including animals, plants and matter
would have intrinsic worth. This implies that nothing in

the universe ought to be treated merely as a means to human ends. The whole of creation ought to be treated with loving care. So adopting a stage four morality is still fundamentally a matter of changing our attitude towards it rather than developing a new content for it.

For the moral and the religious consciousness there should be no conflict between our duties to ourselves and to others, or to nature. But our self-interest and the interests of others, and nature, do not always coincide for us. In stage one these conflicts were resolved in favour of the self. Then "the other" existed only as a means to the agent's pleasure. In stage two, these conflicts were resolved in favour of the other. Then, the agent's will was identical with and subordinate to the will of others, through the social institutions which nurtured him/her, and nature did not have standing in the moral universe. In stage three, these conflicts were resolved sometimes in the favour of the self, sometimes in favour of others or nature, depending on which course of action produced a richer and more harmonious personality. But there are situations, according to Bradley, where these conflicts cannot be resolved, or at least we can't see how they are to be resolved. We find that we must sacrifice ourselves, or others, or nature for the greater good, for the good of creation as a whole. True self-sacrifice (doing good at some great cost to the self), cannot be resolved at stage three, the highest level of morality. It can only be dealt with at stage four, the religious level. There good and evil, in the moral sense, are transformed into a different kind of goodness, which integrates them both: "Both goodness and badness are therefore good, just as in the end falsehood and truth were each found to be true."[62] Just as every judgement is partially true and partially false, so everything we are and do is partially good and partially bad. But this does not mean that moral judgements are relative in an epistemologically vicious sense. The metaphysical doctrine of the degrees of truth, goodness, and reality does not lead to general moral skepticism. In the context in which they are asserted many judgements can be said to be absolutely true or false and many actions absolutely right or wrong. Bradley says:

> Within limits and in their proper place our relative view insists everywhere on the value and on the necessity of absolute judgements, both as to right and wrong and as to error and truth.[63]

James Allard has demonstrated convincingly that Bradley's theory of truth is best expressed as a theory of sufficient reason. A judgement is true, for Bradley, if and only if the argument which the judgement abbreviates is sound.[64] Both truth and falsehood may be true, but they are not true in the same way. Error and falsehood are necessary conditions of the process of seeking truth. They provide part of the dynamics that fuel the search for truth. Nevertheless within that process it is error and falsehood which are to be liquidated, not truth. Although error and falsehood have an understandable place in the larger scheme of things, they have no value by themselves. So too with evil. Both evil and good may be good, but not in the same way. Evil is a necessary condition of the process of self-realization but within the process it is evil, not good, which we aim at obliterating. Although evil may have an understandable place in the larger scheme of things, it has no value by itself. In fact it's existence is parasitic on good, and good can exist without evil. Outside the process of the search for truth, falsehood may be said to contain truth, but inside the process, it is simply falsehood. And outside of morality, evil may be said to contain good, but inside the process of self-development, it is simply evil. The mystical consciousness has absorbed, but not obliterated, the moral consciousness.

Stage four is also the stage of Faith. The religious moral agent must assent to the principle of the sanctity of existence, and the self-sacrifices it implies, on Faith. And Faith is not simply a matter of assenting to an unverified belief or to a belief which cannot be verified.[65] It is a way of existing, for Bradley, not just a way of believing. Nevertheless it is a way of existing which incorporates the belief that the universe, as it exists, is ultimately good.

Stage four is thought by Bradley to be morally better than stage three because it is richer and more harmonious. The agent's moral universe has expanded to include the whole of creation as well as humankind. It makes an attempt to come to terms with the existence of evil itself, a project which is not possible at the moral level. It also tries to come to terms with our inability to solve the conflict between self-development and self-sacrifice. Finally it tries to make sense of supererogatory conduct, which goes beyond the call of moral duty. The ordinary consciousness recognizes the existence of saints and heroes, moral agents whose conduct goes beyond what can be morally required of anyone. The action of saints and heroes is seen as morally desirable but not obligatory. Self-sacrifice is perhaps the most dramatic expression of supererogatory conduct. Stage four makes sense of the heroic virtues in a way not possible even at the highest stages of moral development. It allows the moral agent to grow beyond the moral virtues to the mystical virtues of faith and hope in the fundamental goodness of the universe, and face the reality of his/her finitude.

The nearest analogues to Bradley's moral psychology are to be found in the works of the modern structuralists, e.g., Piaget and Kohlberg.[66] A comparison of Bradley's moral psychology with modern structuralism will help bring out the strengths and weaknesses of his theory. Since Kohlberg's work has generated the most recent debate on structuralism, a comparison of his theory and Bradley's should prove the most useful. Kohlberg, like Bradley, holds that moral development works through a series of distinct stages. For Kohlberg these stages are invariant and appear in the same order in all societies. There is then a uniform moral process which is not culturally relative. Bradley I think is committed to a similar view but he does not explicitly adopt it. He holds, as Kohlberg does, that the content of morality varies from culture to culture and within each of the stages of individual development. But he is committed to the view that the form or structure of each stage is invariant both for individuals and societies. On both theories the same structural development should appear in everyone, irrespective of culture.

The stages identified by Bradley and Kohlberg are broadly similar in both numbers and type.[67] Kohlberg's general divisions of morality are: pre-conventional, conventional and post-conventional (principled). These are roughly the same as Bradley's divisions: egotistic hedonism, institutionalism, and personalism. A summary of Bradley's stages of the moral life is presented in the Appendix, pp. 246-248. In his later works Kohlberg added another higher stage which is roughly similar to Bradley's metaphysical mystical stage.[68] He recognises correctly, as Bradley does, the need to examine morality from religious and metaphysical perspectives. To deal with the problem of the existence of evil and our moral attitudes towards creation as a whole, we have to view the moral process from the outside, as religion and metaphysics does, rather than from within. Neither Kohlberg nor Bradley tried to integrate cognitive and moral development with religious development which also appears to evolve through a series of distinct stages. Had they done so their accounts of the relations between the moral and religious stages would have profited.[69] Kohlberg's comparative cultural studies of moral development have established, with reasonable certainty, that stages one (pre-conventional) and two (conventional) are universal. But he has been less successful with stage three (post-conventional, principled).[70] Part of his failure can be traced to his analysis of stage three in terms of the values of a liberal democracy. These values are more likely to be found in countries with histories of liberal democratic governments, like the United States and Canada, than ones which have no democratic traditions. Common sense and the known history of civilizations would indicate that stage four (religious, metaphysical, mystic) could be universal. Perhaps the personalism of Bradley's stage three would find its expression in many cultures in a religious rather than a secular form. If this were the case, cross-cultured studies would then support the universality of Bradley's stages.

Kohlberg divides each of his three main stages into two sub-stages, hence he posits six distinct stages of development instead of three, as Bradley and most other

structuralists do.[71] The subdivisions made in the
pre-conventional and conventional stages are of little
importance for a comparison with Bradley's theory. They
simply refine the main stages but are not fundamentally
different. The subdivisions made in the post-conventional or principled stage are important because it is in
this stage that Bradley and Kohlberg differ the most from
each other. Kohlberg divides his post-conventional stage
into two further sub-stages. Both stage five and stage
six are based on individual assent to a universal first
principle which orders moral reasoning for that stage.
In stage five the principle of social utility is dominant. In this stage the rightness or wrongness of
actions is determined by the actual consequences of the
action. In stage six the principles of justice (fair-
ness/equality) is dominant. In this stage the rightness
or wrongness is based on consistency with the principles
of justice. Stage five is clearly utilitarian, while the
highest stage is Kantian, at least as seen through the
eyes of the modern philosophers John Rawls and Richard
Hare.[72] For Bradley moral reasoning in the third, or
personalist, stage also operates in terms of universal
principles like utility, justice and respect for persons.
However no single principle has epistemological priority
over the others. The goal here is to produce a comprehensive and unified system of morality and the ultimate
criteria to be used are richness and integration.
Bradley, then, cannot be accused of presupposing in his
theory a set of values implicit in his own culture, as
Kohlberg can. Bradley is not culture-blind.

For both Kohlberg and Bradley, each stage represents
a structural whole in which cognitive, emotive and moral
elements are integrated. For Kohlberg the cognitive
element is dominant. It is the epistemology which

provides the structural unity for each stage. The emotive aspect and the development of moral character have only a subsidiary role to play in the system. In fact Kohlberg is quite hostile to the theory of virtue.[73] As a result he has often been criticized for neglecting these aspects of morality.[74] For Bradley, emotion is as important for moral development as thought is. In each stage, a new level of emotional, as well as cognitive, maturity is reached. New needs, as well as new cognitive capacities, appear at each stage. In stage two, for example, the desire to pursue truth for its own sake arises, and thought ceases to be the slave of other passions and is now a separate desire:

> Reality or Good, will now be the satisfaction of all the wants of our nature, and theoretical truth will be the perceptions and ideas which directly satisfy one of those wants, and so indirectly make part of the general satisfaction.[75]

The truth satisfies our desire to know, even though truth is not that desire satisfied. Bradley is also concerned with the theory of virtue. In fact the whole process of moral development is one which moves in the direction of perfect virtue: ". . . goodness is the realization by an individual of his own perfection. . . ."[76] Bradley's theory of moral development then is not open to the same criticisms which can be directed at Kohlberg's theory. Nor is Bradley open to another standard criticism of Kohlberg. It is often argued that Kohlberg's post-conventional stage six is biased in favour of Kantian ethics and against utilitarian and other well developed philosophical theories. R. S. Peters puts the point aptly:

> He suffers from the rather touching belief that a Kantian type of morality, represented in modern times most notably by Hare and Rawls, is the only one. He fails to grasp that utilitarianism, in which the principle of justice is problematic, is an alternative type of morality, and that people such as Winch have put forward a morality of integrity in which the principle of universalizability is problematic.[77]

Moral reasoning for Bradley, at its highest levels, is a process of synthesizing competing values in ways which allow them all to be expressed. It is both consequentialist and non-consequentialist, incorporating what is valuable in both utilitarianism and Kantianism. It is both principled and contextual. A growing system in which universal and particular dance together in harmony. It is true that for Bradley the principle of individuation, which consciously controls thought and morality at the highest levels, expresses values through the criteria of richness and integration. Kohlberg also uses these values, as Bradley does, to show why the later stages of moral development are better intellectually and morally than the earlier stages, and to explain the psychological dynamics which push moral agents to higher stages of development. For both Kohlberg and Bradley, it is psychological tension which powers moral development.[78] But Kohlberg does not use them, as Bradley does, to express the highest stages of moral thought. Had he done so he would not have been so vulnerable to Peters' argument from moral pluralism. Since the principle of self-realization is not morally neutral, then Bradley's moral psychology cannot be morally neutral. It implicitly recommends, as well as explicitly explaining, moral values. To accept the view that there are no morally neutral moral psychologies would not be a serious setback for Bradley. He could have argued, although he did not, that the hypothesis of self-realization still makes more sense of moral experience than any proposed alternative, even if it is not morally neutral. To reject the idea of moral and epistemological neutrality would imply that ethical theory has a richer role to play in practical ethics and logic than Bradley would have accepted. Kohlberg, unlike Bradley, was optimistic about applying ethical and psychological theory to moral practise. Indeed his prime interest was to develop adequate programs of moral education, especially in democratic societies.[79] In this he is surely right. Ethical theory and ethical practise are different aspects of our moral experience. You cannot have one without the other. Ethical theory has a positive as well as a negative relation to practical ethics. Bradley reluctantly accepted the negative relation of theory to practise, but not the positive. To accept the positive would mean that moral education should place emphasis on developing the creative insights which are required to solve moral dilemmas at the highest levels of moral reasoning. But it would also imply a recognition that there is no agreement among either moral philosophers, or moral psychologists, as to which ethical or psychological theory is the best. An implication which would in any case be consistent with Bradley's theory of moral development, as it preserves the personalism of the later stages of moral growth. The goal of ethical theory would still be to understand moral experience rather than to recommend how people should conduct themselves. Its aim would still be theoretical as well as practical. A good ethical theory will still be one which satisfies intellectually as well as practically. If an ethical theory doesn't do this then it will have bad results when applied to practise.

Kohlberg has recently been criticized by Carol Gilligan for having a male, as well as a moral, bias in his work.[80] She argues that Kohlberg's highest levels of morality express a masculine rather than a feminine set of values. The values emphasized by Kohlberg, like justice, equality and universality, are values inculcated into the men, not the women, in our society. Kohlberg overlooks the values of caring, concern for others and loved ones, and the appreciation of the uniqueness of context, which characterize the female moral experience. There are two, not one moral experiences, a female and a male one. By ignoring women's moral development, Kohlberg misrepresents the higher levels of moral reasoning. Bradley would not, I suspect, accept that we have two distinct moral experiences. There is only one moral universe which has different aspects. Bradley's highest levels have both masculine and feminine elements which need to be integrated in each individual, without either being dominant. He does admit that intuitive understanding, which is the highest type of moral reasoning, is often more fully developed in women than in men. In this he anticipates Gilligan's findings:

> And I think I may add (though I do it in
> fear) that women in general are remarkable
> for the fineness of their moral

perceptions, and the quickness of their judgements, and yet are or (let me save myself by saying) 'maybe' not remarkable for corresponding discursive ability.[81]

Bradley does not think that women's intellects are completely intuitive nor men's completely discursive. But he does think that in practical matters women are superior in judgement to men, because their intuitive understanding is more highly developed.[82] In any case Gilligan's criticisms would not be relevant for Bradley's moral psychology as they might be for Kohlberg's.

F. H. Bradley wrote at a time when psychology was developing as a special discipline independent of philosophy. The methodology which the new science adopted was essentially experimental. It modelled itself on the natural sciences. Just as the natural sciences could not progress until they had become morally and metaphysically neutral, so psychology would not progress until it had done the same. For natural science this meant shifting from teleological explanations of natural events to mechanical ones, and psychology followed their lead. The new science which separated from philosophy was experimental, morally neutral and mechanistic.

The specialization of psychology, and the other social sciences, during the nineteenth century had good and bad consequences, but for moral psychology the result was largely bad. On the one hand, the way psychological theories were verified was improved. Hypotheses were now tested by controlled observation as well as against data which had been systematically collected. Kohlberg's work benefitted to some extent from the use of this methodology.[83] Bradley's method was perhaps more piecemeal, but no less important. He drew his data from introspection, from his own and others' moral experience, and from his comparisons between animal and human behaviour. The "common moral consciousness" provided the data base for the later stages in which moral agency and theoretical reasoning were well developed. The comparison between animal and human intelligence helped provide insights into the earlier stages when moral agency and moral reasoning were less developed:

> In the disparaging estimate, if it is disparaging, I may seem to have formed of animal intelligence, I may say that I have done nothing but estimate myself. Without doubting my own title to rationality, I observe in myself at my less conscious moments those processes and those feelings which, with certain exceptions seem to explain the acts of the lowest creatures. And these processes are united to my highest functions by one steady advance of one single principle, first unconscious, then reflective, but always reasonable.[84]

Specialization tended to isolate psychology from ethics and ethics from psychology. Modern psychology tends to look at human beings as natural objects governed by the laws of efficient causality, while the best moral philosophy, tends to look at them as moral agents governed by laws of teleology. Kohlberg is one of the few great modern psychologists who recognizes that teleology and science are not necessarily incompatible. He, like Bradley, sees that if psychology is going to be relevant for morality, it must be consistent with and be able to account for moral agency. He also agrees with Bradley that mechanistic psychologies, like behaviorism which are the modern experimental forms of utilitarian association psychology, cannot deal adequately with moral agency or the higher cognitive functions of human beings.[85] Specialization also tends to isolate ethics from its data base in ordinary moral experience and in the systematic investigations into morality undertaken by the social sciences. It turns in upon itself and becomes radically autonomous. On the specialist view ethics is logically independent of the social sciences and ordinary moral experience. It should come as no surprise that the autonomous view of ethics finds its fullest expression in the ethics of G. E. Moore, the author of the naturalistic fallacy.

Moore thought that the alternative to accepting the naturalistic fallacy, and divorcing ethics from science and metaphysics, was a specious form of reductionism. Morality was reduced to science, metaphysics or theology. The utilitarian reduced ethics to a branch of individual psychology. Idealists like Bradley reduced it to a branch of metaphysics. These reductions were so plainly false to Moore that he found it difficult to see how any rational person could accept them.[86] In order to escape the dilemma which the naturalistic fallacy posed for ethics, Moore adopted the view that fundamental moral principles must be self-evidently true. Ethical thinking was a matter of seeing that certain states of affairs possessed the non-natural property of "goodness." For judgements of intrinsic value no relevant evidence could be produced to support them:

> It becomes plain that, for answers to the
> first question (what ought to exist for
> its own sake), no relevant evidence

whatever can be adduced: from no other truth, except themselves alone, can it be inferred that they are either true or false.[87]

Moore's intuitionism has been abandoned by most contemporary ethicists, because the system provided no adequate way of resolving conflicts of intuition. If two equally well-informed, mature persons disagree concerning an important moral matter there would be no rational way of resolving the issue between them. Each would have to claim that the other was morally blind, i.e., simply didn't perceive that the state of affairs in question did possess the non-natural property of goodness. It is true that the moral sensibilities, like aesthetic sensibilities, need to be educated in order to function properly. Just as our initial encounters with complex works of art, like Beethoven's late string quartets or Picasso's later paintings, may be bewildering and annoying to us (we may even find them incomprehensible or ugly), so our initial perception of complex moral problems may be equally disquieting. And just as closer inspection of an aesthetic object (by trying to hear or see them properly), allows us to understand and appreciate them better, so by more careful inspection of moral situations do we come to understand them better. There are contexts in which the use of phrases like "moral insight," "moral blindness," or "He just doesn't see that what he is doing is morally wrong" are appropriate. Nevertheless the basic criticism of Moore's intuitionism is sound. The system really does not provide an adequate way of resolving conflicts of intuition as Bradley's theory does. Appeals to self-evidence are often as Mill noted simply appeals to fashion and prejudice in morals, a way to avoid argument, rather than to establish moral judgements.

Moore's defense of a logically self-sufficient ethics was widely and well received in the English-speaking world during the first half of this century, by both philosophers and non-philosophers alike. One could well ask why such an obviously inadequate theory of moral reasoning was ever so widely accepted. Outside of the sheer logical ingenuity of the arguments Moore advanced, there seems to be only one likely explanation. Moore's moral philosophy recommended itself in different ways to narrow specialist groups which were growing antagonistic to each other: the philosophical, artistic, and scientific communities. The theory was readily accepted by the scientific community because the majority of practicing scientists believed that their work was morally neutral. The scientist deals with facts and nothing but facts, and moral judgements were expelled from the laboratories. The theory could be even more happily embraced by the majority of practicing social scientists, partly because the social sciences were new, but mostly because it was widely held that the social sciences had to be morally neutral in order to be truly scientific. The theory would have natural appeal to the artistic community, because of the sharp separation of science from morals and because of the close parallel Moore drew between moral and aesthetic judgements. For the artist, it would be odd to claim that one had, for instance, to have mastered Darwin's The Origin of the Species and The Descent of Man in order to understand the difference between right and wrong. The artist has frequently been credited with possessing moral as well as aesthetic insight. A kind of insight not unlike that which Moore required for discerning the intrinsic value of particular states of affairs. If Moore was right, the artists could go on their lonely, individual, intuitive journeys, dealing with the fundamental human problems of beauty and morality, happily ignorant of science, philosophy and community. The scientific and the artistic communities could even admire each other from the safe isolation of their specialist jurisdictions. It was a form of intellectual apartheid which separated the strands of our intellectual life in the wrong way and with equally damaging results for the culture.

Moral philosophers, too, could perform their complicated and subtle conceptual analyses, weaving gossamer moral systems, without concerning themselves with the relevance of their work for the psychological or sociological realities of human life. Moral philosophy, like science, became morally neutral. It ceased to have relevance for life. It is obvious that Moore never intended that moral philosophy should become devoid of significance for life. Why would he have bothered to write a chapter in Principia Ethica entitled, "Ethics in Relation to Conduct," in which he outlines his positive, if stage two, claim that we are likely to produce the most good if we act in conformity with the established moral rules of the society in which we live?[88] Nor would he have written the final chapter on "The Ideal," in which he argued that personal relations and the appreciation of beauty possessed the most intrinsic value:

> By far the most valuable things which we know or can imagine, are certain states of consciousness, which may be roughly described as the pleasures of human intercourse and the enjoyment of beautiful objects.[89]

Nevertheless his work did result in ethics becoming irrelevant for life. It certainly had this effect on many of his disciples, especially those artists, writers, and scientists, who were members of the Bloomsbury Group, which played such an important role in English cultural history during the Edwardian era. No profound insight into the influence G. E. Moore had on the formation of the culture of Bloomsbury is necessary to perceive how quickly they emptied Moore's moral philosophy of its practical relevance. John Maynard Keynes writes:

> We accepted Moore's religion, so to speak, and discarded his morals. Indeed, in our opinion, one of the greatest advantages of his religion, was that it made morals unnecessary--meaning by 'religion' one's attitude towards oneself and the ultimate and by 'morals' one's attitude towards the outside world and the intermediate.[90]

The religion the Bloomsbury Group received from Moore was a purely intellectual one, which focused on personal love, the admiration of beauty, and the pursuit of knowledge. It was, according to Keynes, essentially otherworldly and excessively rationalistic. In the hands of Bloomsbury, Moore's moral philosophy was transformed into an irrelevant rationalism. As Keynes remarked:

> Indeed we combined a dogmatic treatment as to the nature of experience with a method of handling it which was extravagantly scholastic.[91]

Moore's disciples became dogmatic and unworldly rationalists who adopted moral postures, the favourite being what Leonard Woolf described as "a strident individualism,"[92] but who had no real interest in justifying their morality or in relating it to the moral traditions from which it had developed. They lacked moral seriousness and reverence, as D. H. Lawrence had observed:

> To hear these young people talk really fills me with a black fury: they talk endlessly, but endlessly--and never, never a good thing said. They are cased each in a hard little shell of his own and out of this they talk words. There is never, for one second, any outgoing of feeling and no reverence, not a crumb or grain of reverence. I cannot stand it. I will not have people like this--I had rather be alone. They made me dream of a beetle that bites a scorpion. But I killed it--a very large beetle. I scotched it and it ran off--but I came on it again, and killed it. It is this horror of little swarming selves I can't stand.[93]

The radical individualism of Bloomsbury too frequently degenerated into a shallow egoism which replaced genuine objective standards of taste and morals with the in-group standards of a self-appointed cultural oligarchy.[94] True, these are pathological developments of Moore's intuitionism within the Bloomsbury culture. There were non-pathological developments as well. As Leonard Woolf has pointed out, Moore also helped the young Edwardians cast off the pall of an outmoded and repressive Victorian morality and move them towards a rediscovery of the value of personal, sexual, and political freedom.[95] The revolt against traditional morality, however, too often became a revolt against community as such, and a movement towards moral anarchy. Nevertheless the revolt against Victorian conventions prevented many of the Bloomsbury group from falling victim to the dark totalitarianism which lurked in the shadows of Lawrence's cosmic vision.[96] Still the pathological developments of systems of thought frequently give us important clues about the structural weaknesses in the systems. Systems of thought tend to break down in idiocyncratic ways. They create their own aberrations, their familiar lunacies. As Jean Paul Sartre's ethics created the pale, gaunt parodies of the committed existentialist, who hung about the Parisian cafés in post-war France.

Moore's intuitionism, when it becomes pathological, makes ethics irrelevant for life. This is borne out not only by the developments of it within Bloomsbury culture, but also by developments within professional philosophy as well. R. M. Hare is probably correct in suggesting that it was Moore's intuitionism which led to the regrettable tendency in contemporary moral philosophy to devote itself to the analysis of moral language rather than to understanding morality.[97] A return to the perspective of F. H. Bradley's idealism could help cure modern moral philosophy of its pathological aversion to lived moral experience, at both the theoretical and practical levels.

Chapter V: The Stages of The Moral Life

1   F. H. Bradley, Ethical Studies, pp. 160-344.

2   F. H. Bradley, Ibid. The quote read, "his function as an organ in the social organism," in the first edition (1876). But the was changed to a in the second edition (1927). The change is important, because the theory is no longer committed to the idea of statism, i.e., right and wrong are determined by the state.

3   H. Sidgwick, Mind (O.S., Vol. 1, 1876), pp. 545-549.

4   F. H. Bradley, Ethical Studies, p. 178.

5   F. H. Bradley, Ibid, especially pp. 280-303.

6   F. H. Bradley, Ibid., p. 190 cf; p. 178 cf; Principles of Logic, p. 511.

7   F. H. Bradley, The Principles of Logic, p. 29.

8   These are my names, not Bradley's, but they are a convenient way to focus on key aspects of the stages of development. Also Bradley doesn't give a precise number of stages. He simply describes a series of them, among which it is possible to discern at least these four.

9   F. H. Bradley, "Association and Thought," Collected Essays, p. 216.

10 F. H. Bradley, Ethical Studies, p. 281.

11 F. H. Bradley, "Association and Thought," pp. 220-225.

12 F. H. Bradley, Appearance and Reality, p. 381 (footnote 1).

13 F. H. Bradley, The Principles of Logic, p. 502.

14 F. H. Bradley, Ibid., p. 504.

15 F. H. Bradley, Ibid, p. 29.

16   F; H. Bradley, The Principles of Logic p. 34.

17   F. H. Bradley, Ibid., p. 29.

18   F. H. Bradley, Appearance and Reality, p. 381
     (footnote 1).

19   F. H. Bradley, The Principles of Logic, p. 31; cf.
     R. Manser, Bradley's Logic, pp. 60-78.

20   F. H. Bradley, Ibid., p. 506; cf. pp. 30-31.

21   F. H. Bradley, Ibid., p. 506.

22   F. H. Bradley, Ethical Studies, p. 263.

23   F. H. Bradley, Ibid., p. 285.

24   F. H. Bradley, Ibid., p. 284.

25   F. H. Bradley, The Principles of Logic, p. 29.

26   F. H. Bradley, Appearance and Reality, p. 9.

27   F. H. Bradley, The Principles of Logic, p. 31.

28   F. H. Bradley, The Principles of Logic, p. 31.

29   F. H. Bradley, Ibid., p. 506.

30   F. H. Bradley, Ethical Studies, p. 285.

31   F. H. Bradley, Ibid., p. 285.

32   F. H. Bradley, Ibid., p. 287.

33   F. H. Bradley, Ibid., p. 286.

34   F. H. Bradley, Ibid., p. 286.

35   F. H. Bradley, The Principles of Logic, p. 37.

36   F. H. Bradley, Ibid., p. 2.

37   F. H. Bradley, Ibid., p. 85.   The brackets are mine.

38   F. H. Bradley, Ibid., p. 506.

39   F. H. Bradley, Ethical Studies, p. 293.

40   F. H. Bradley, Ibid., p. 203.

41   F. H. Bradley, Ibid., pp. 203-204.

42   F. H. Bradley, Ibid., p. 205.

43   F. H. Bradley, "The Definition of Will (II),"
     Collected Essays, p. 525.

44   F. H. Bradley, Ethical Studies, pp. 204-205.

45   F. H. Bradley, Ibid., p. 190.

46   F. H. Bradley, Ibid., p. 189.

47 Cf. my The Moral Question: Ethical Theory, pp. 9-14.

48 F. H. Bradley, Ethical Studies, p. 189.

49 F. H. Bradley, Ibid., p. 313.

50 F. H. Bradley, Ibid., p. 191 (footnote 1).

51 F. H. Bradley, Ibid., p. 314.

52 F. H. Bradley, Appearance and Reality, p. 178.

53 F. H. Bradley, Ethical Studies, p. 314.

54 F. H. Bradley, Ibid., p. 316; Appearance and Reality (footnote), pp. 388-389.

55 F. H. Bradley, Ibid., p. 325.

56 F. H. Bradley, Ibid., p. 335.

57 F. H. Bradley, Ibid., p. 336.

58 F. H. Bradley, Ibid., p. 338.

59 F. H. Bradley, Ibid., p. 339.

60 F. H. Bradley, Appearance and Reality, p. 390.

61 F. H. Bradley, "Is Self-Sacrifice an Enigma?," Collected Essays, p. 130.

62 F. H. Bradley, Appearance and Reality, p. 390.

63 F. H. Bradley, Essays on Truth and Reality, p. 266.

64 James Allard, "Bradley's Principle of Sufficient Reason," The Philosophy of F. H. Bradley, p. 174.

65 F. H. Bradley, Ethical Studies, p. 326; Appearance and Reality, p. 392.

66 Jean Piaget, The Moral Judgement of the Child (London, 1932), and Lawrence Kohlberg, Essays on Moral Development, Vols. I, II, and III (Harper, 1981-82).

67 Kohlberg, Essays on Moral Development, Vol. I, pp. 409-412.

68 Kohlberg, Ibid, pp. 311-372.

69 E. V. Sullivan, Kohlberg's Structuralism (O.I.S.E., Toronto, 1977), p. 37.

70 Kohlberg, Essays on Moral Development, pp. 115-130.

71   Kohlberg, "The Cognitive-Developmental Approach to Moral Education," <u>Moral Education</u>, ed. by Purpel and Ryan (Berkeley, 1976), p. 177.

72   John Rawls, <u>A Theory of Justice</u>, Harvard, 1971, and R. M. Hare, <u>Freedom and Reason</u> (Oxford, 1963).

73   Kohlberg, <u>Essays on Moral Development</u>, Vol. I, pp. 29-48.

74   R. S. Peters, "Moral Development: A Plea for Pluralism," <u>Cognitive Development and Epistemology</u>, Mischel (Academic Press, 1971), and "Why Doesn't Lawrence Kohlberg Do His Homework?," Purpel and Ryan, <u>Moral Education</u>, pp. 288-290; cf. E. V. Sullivan, <u>Kohlberg's Structuralism</u>, p. 15.

75   F. H. Bradley, <u>Essays on Truth and Reality</u>, p. 98, cf. <u>Appearance and Reality</u>, p. 356 (footnote 2). For the importance of emotion in Bradley's metaphysics see James Bradley, "The Critique of Pure Feeling," <u>Process Studies</u> (Vol. 14, No. 4, 1985), pp. 253-264.

76   F. H. Bradley, <u>Appearance and Reality</u>, p. 367.

77   R. S. Peters, <u>Moral Education</u>, pp. 288-289; cf. E. V. Sullivan, <u>Kohlberg's Structuralism</u>, pp. 6-14, and Brian Crittendin, <u>Form and Content in Moral Education</u> (O.I.S.E., Toronto, 1975), pp. 14-28.

78   Kohlberg, Ibid., p. 178.

79   Kohlberg, <u>Essays in Moral Development</u>, Vol. I, pp. 1-96. For a discussion of the problems of moral education in a democracy see my article, "Moral Education," <u>The Canadian Forum</u> (May, 1984), pp. 16ff.

80   Carol Gilligan, <u>In a Different Voice</u> (Harvard, 1982).

81   F. H. Bradley, <u>Ethical Studies</u>, p. 195.

82   F. H. Bradley, Ibid., p. 195, footnote 2.

83   Kohlberg, <u>Essays on Moral Development</u>, Vol. I, pp. 115-130.

84   F. H. Bradley, <u>The Principles of Logic</u>, p. 510.

85   Kohlberg, <u>Essays on Moral Development</u>, Vol. I, pp. 101-105.

86   G. E. Moore, <u>Ethics</u> (Oxford, 1912), pp. 54-55.

87   G. E. Moore, <u>Principia Ethica</u>, p. viii. The phrase in the brackets is mine.

88   G. E. Moore, Ibid., pp. 142-182.

89   G. E. Moore, Ibid., p. 189.

90   John Maynard Keynes, "My Early Beliefs," in S. P. Rosenbaum, <u>The Bloomsbury Group</u> (University of Toronto Press, 1975), p. 52.

91   John Maynard Keynes, Ibid., p. 55.

92   Leonard Woolf, "Cambridge Friends and Influences," <u>The Bloomsbury Group</u>, pp. 92-109.

93   D. H. Lawrence in a letter to Lady Ottoline Morrell, quoted by David Garrett in "Lawrence and Bloomsbury," <u>The Bloomsbury Group</u>, p. 368.

94   Cf. F. R. Leavis, "Keynes, Lawrence and Cambridge," <u>The Common Pursuit</u> (Chatto and Windus, 1953), pp. 255-260.

95   Leonard Woolf, "Cambridge Friends and Influences," <u>The Bloomsbury Group</u>, pp. 103-109.

96   Bertrand Russell, "D. H. Lawrence," <u>Portraits From Memory and Other Essays</u> (Allen & Unwin, London, 1956), pp. 104-108.

97   R. M. Hare, "Broad's Approach to Moral Philosophy," <u>Essays on Philosophical Method</u> (Macmillan, 1971) p. 2.

CHAPTER VI
Personal and Social Morality

In Essay 5 of <u>Ethical Studies</u>, Bradley develops a refutation of radical individualism, the view that individuals are ontologically independent of the social groups (institutions) to which they belong and that social groups (institutions) are ontologically dependent on the individuals which compose them:

> The family, society, the state, and generally every community of men, consists of individuals, and there is nothing in them real except the individuals. Individuals have made them, and make them, by placing themselves and by standing in certain relations. The individuals are real by themselves and it is because of them that the relations are real. They made them, they are real in them, not because of them, and they would be just as real out of them. The whole is the mere sum of its parts, and the parts are as real away from the whole as they are within the whole.[1]

The refutation of radical individualism plays a central role in Bradley's moral philosophy. The belief that conformity to an existing moral code is the heart of Bradley's ethics rests to a large extent on this fact. This view wrongly presupposes that it is sociology, not psychology, which is the foundation of ethical idealism. It is not, however, supported by the facts. It is true that Bradley held that utilitarian and Kantian ethics presuppose sociologies as well as psychologies. In fact their sociologies have more in common than their psychologies, because both rest on forms of radical individualism. Utilitarians and Kantians, however, develop their sociologies differently because they see human nature differently. They work out of radically different psychologies. For the Utilitarian man is a rational pleasure (happiness)-seeker; for the Kantian man is a rational virtue-seeker. We can call the Utilitarian view "hedonistic individualism," and the Kantian view "moral individualism." For the utilitarian morality is not natural to the individual. It arises out of inter-action between rational pleasure-seekers. Some but not all of these relationships are contractual. Morality for the Utilitarian is essentially social. Someone living on a desert island would have no need of morality. For the utilitarian, to say "X is a duty/obligatory/ required," is to say "we can be legitimately coerced to do or refrain from doing X." If we fail to do X then sanctions of some kind can be legitimately brought to bear on us, to force us to do what is required of us. As J. S. Mill said:

> It is part of the notion of duty in every one of its forms that a person may rightfully be compelled to fulfil it. Duty is a thing which may be exacted from a person, as one exacts a debt. Unless we think that it may be exacted from him, we do not call it his duty.[2]

These sanctions can be either legal or social. If I fail to repay a debt, legal action can be taken against me. If I fail to keep a promise, the promisee has a right to be annoyed with me, or my social conscience will plague me. Morality is equated with that sphere of life where social control of conduct is appropriate. Acts are morally significant only when they affect the interests of others. The utilitarians draw a sharp distinction between a public moral world and a private amoral world. Hence all moral problems can be reduced to the question of whether social control is appropriate or not. The fundamental moral question for a utilitarian is to decide whether an act is public or private. An act is considered private if it does not significantly affect the interests of anyone other than the agent; otherwise it is public. For the utilitarian who sticks with his definition of duty there are no duties to the self, only duties to others. Suicide, for example, would be immoral only if it involved a breach of our duty to others. If there were no specific duties to others it would be morally permissible to commit suicide if one wanted to. Suicide is morally permissible on utilitarian grounds so long as no one else is harmed. Once the question of moral obligation to others is settled there are no other moral questions to ask. There are only prudential questions about individual happiness. What we do with our lives is primarily a private and not a public matter. Suicide is essentially a private act which concerns each individual first, hence social control of suicide would be inappropriate.

The utilitarian would likely argue that we ought to have a "right to die," or be able to take our own life whenever we want to. They would also argue that aiding suicide, as well as attempted suicide, should be decriminalized. It should not be a criminal offence for a physician to prescribe poison pills to a rational patient who requested them. For the utilitarian, life is only worth living if it possesses a certain quality, if it provides a satisfactory balance of pleasure (happiness) over pain (unhappiness/suffering). Life or existence has no intrinsic value for the utilitarian. In considering suicide the main question becomes whether the agent has a hope for pleasurable or happy life. This is not a moral question for the consistent utilitarian, but a matter of personal preference. Once settled negatively, there is no reason why one should not commit suicide. Not to do so would be irrational. The Utilitarian is also committed to the view that we should have legal and moral rights to active, as well as passive, voluntary euthanasia. There are situations in which people really have no rational hope for a happy life, e.g., many terminally ill patients are in this state. What upsets the opponents of the "right to die" legislation is that removing suicide from the moral arena will undermine the value we place on the principle of sanctity of human life. The difference between voluntary and involuntary euthanasia is difficult to draw on utilitarian grounds because the actual consequences, the relief from suffering, are the same in both situations. Shouldn't the comatose or the mentally incompetent (the mentally handicapped and newborns) have the same rights as others? A utilitarian defense of the "right to die" undermines the principle of sanctity of life.

For the Kantian the individual is a rational virtue-seeker, hence morality is natural to him. It is innate and does not arise out of a social process. Morality for the Kantian is essentially private. For the Kantian to be obligated means to act under self-imposed laws. As Kant says: "Obligation is the necessity of a free action under a categorical imperative of reason."[3] No one can be compelled by others to recognize moral obligations, or to carry out externally imposed moral requirements.

Agents can be forced to produce consequences others require, but this is to act in conformity to duty and not out of duty, and only the latter is moral. The moral man does his duty because it is the morally right thing to do, and not because of any rewards it may bring or any punishment it may avoid. The utilitarian and Kantian concepts of duty are radically different from each other. The former is socially defined, the latter is personally defined. A utilitarian theory of obligation is similar to that found in a stage two morality, while the Kantian theory of obligation is more appropriate for a stage three morality.

The Kantians, like the Utilitarians, draw a sharp distinction between our public and private worlds. But for the Kantian, it is the private world which is moral, while the public world is amoral. It is the individuals who moralize society, not the society which moralizes individuals or imposes a morality on them. The state and its legal system, society and its social system, is created by interaction between individuals who pursue virtue. A social contract between rational moral agents will of course be radically different than one between two rational pleasure (happiness)-seekers. For one thing it will be based on the principle of respect for persons, rather than on the principle of utility. The system of rights developed from the former will be different from that derived from the latter. In the Kantian system, the fundamental goal would be the maximization of individual freedom and the minimization of social control. The basic axiom of a Kantian theory of rights would be "do as you ought so long as you don't interfere with the freedom of other moral agents." Kant says:

> A constitution allowing the greatest
> possible human freedom in accordance with
> laws by which the freedom of each is made
> to be consistent with that of all oth-
> ers--I do not speak of the greatest
> happiness, for this will follow of it-
> self--is at any rate a necessary idea,
> which must be taken as fundamental not
> only in first projecting a constitution
> but in all its laws.[4]

For the Utilitarian the goal of the system would be the maximization of pleasure (happiness) and the minimization of pain (suffering). The basic axiom of a utilitarian theory of rights would be "do as you please so long as you don't harm others." Utilitarians have, of course, always been strong defenders of freedom but the freedom they cherish is freedom _from_ morality, not freedom _for_ morality. A theory of rights, adequate to justify individual liberty, does not come easy, if at all, to the Utilitarians. For example, it is difficult to see how a Utilitarian could decide in favour of freedom when it conflicts with providing food and other necessities of life, as often happens in underdeveloped countries. Basing a theory of rights on negative utilities (the minimization of suffering), as the Utilitarians must do, will not protect the theory from collapsing into an undesirable form of paternalism, which denies the reality and the freedom of the moral agent.

Although the Kantian believes in a kind of absolute moral freedom, he, like the Utilitarian, accepts a form of social control. We need law to protect us from evil and to punish the guilty. Social control is necessary because human beings are not perfect moral agents. We are not always able to overcome the desires which lead us astray. Weakness of will affects all of us and because it does, evil flourishes. Hence law and social control are a natural extension of the moral order. Both Kantians and Utilitarians believe we have a duty to obey the law, but the grounds for the duty are different. For the Utilitarian the duty to obey the law is based on the belief that an ordered society is essential for everyone's pleasure or happiness. Without the security provided by law and social order, everyone's pleasure or happiness would be endangered. Society would dissolve into what Hobbes called "the state of nature":

> . . . during the time men live without a common power to keep them all in awe, they are in that condition which is called war, and such a war as is of every man against every man.[5]

For the Kantian our duty to obey the law is based on the belief that it expresses and protects the fundamental values of the moral order, values like sanctity of human life and respect for persons. We have no obligation to obey an immoral law. So whether we ought to obey the law or ignore it will depend on the value it represents. With suicide, for example, the matter is fairly straight-forward. The Kantians believe that suicide is immoral because it is inconsistent with the principles of sanctity of human life and respect for persons. Since human beings are rational moral agents, all human life is intrinsically valuable no matter what its quality. Respect for life implies a strict rule against the taking of a human life, against murder. There are few, if any, exceptions to it. Since suicide is a breach of the rule against murder, it is self-murder, it would be morally wrong. As would aiding suicide. Suicide is also inconsistent with principle of respect for persons. Because each person is a moral agent they automatically possess intrinsic value. To destroy what is intrinsically valuable is morally wrong. As Kant says:

> . . . a man is still obligated to preserve his life simply because he is a person and must therefore recognize a duty to himself (and a strict one at that).[6]

Kantians, then, would not approve of someone taking his/her own life in order to avoid suffering. They would strongly oppose active voluntary euthanasia and would not want to decriminalize aiding suicide. They would be willing to allow some forms of passive voluntary euthanasia, for example, where medical treatment is stopped in hopeless cases, and the patient is allowed to die a natural death. For the Kantian we do have legal and social obligations but these are based on power, not right. We can be coerced to conform to the letter of the law out of fear of punishment, but we are not morally obligated to obey the law unless it is just or moral. In the end all duties are really duties to the self. If we had no duty to pursue personal virtue, we would have no duty to pursue social virtue. As Kant says:

> Suppose there were no such duties (duties to the self). Then there would be no duties at all, not even external ones. For I cannot recognize myself as bound to others except insofar as I bind myself at the same time.[7]

If the Utilitarian reduces all duties to duties to others, the Kantian reduces all duties to duties to the self. For the former, private morality ceases to exist, for the latter public morality vanishes. According to Bradley, if you start with moral individualism you cannot get to community. The moral rules of a community are the rules in practice. They cannot be merely abstract ideals which ought to be in practice. A purely inner-directed morality which has no implications for society is meaningless:

> The good, we may be informed, is morality, and morality is inward. It does not consist in the attainment of a mere result, either outside the self or even within it. For a result must depend on, and be conditioned by, what is naturally given, and for natural defects or advantages a man is not responsible.[8]

For the Kantian, the rightness or wrongness of an action is determined by the motive of conscientiousness. It does not depend on the actual consequences, hence anyone can be perfectly moral without realizing any actual good. As long as our motives are pure, we are good. We cannot be held responsible for the unintended consequences of our actions. But in real life we are often held both legally and morally responsible for the unintended consequences of our actions. In law, for example, the idea of medical negligence would make little sense unless physicians could be held responsible for the unintended consequences of their actions. The surgeon who operates intends to cure, not kill, at least we hope so. So if something goes wrong and the patient dies, the

death was unintentional. The physician would not be
charged with murder, but he could be charged with negligence, if his surgical practice was inadequate. And even
if he escaped the law, he could be held morally responsible for the death of his patient. The physician is
morally and legally required to possess a certain excel-
lence. We can, then, be held responsible for the kind of
person we are as well as for the things we do. A careless physician is just not morally acceptable. Nor is a
drunken car driver. Thus the inner and outer dimensions
of morality are both essential to it. You cannot have
private morality without public morality, and you cannot
have public morality without private morality. As
Bradley says:

> . . . moral institutions are carcasses
> without personal morality and personal
> morality apart from social institutions is
> an unreality, a soul without a body.[9]

Once the private and public aspects of morality are
divorced from each other, as both Utilitarians and
Kantians tend to do, you can never get them united again.
And both ethical theories will account for only one side
of morality. Morality exists at both the personal and
the social levels, and an adequate ethical theory must
account for both aspects of the moral life. Hedonistic
and moral individualism are inadequate theories because
they presuppose radical individualism. On this theory
social groups are seen as collections of externally
related individuals:

> What are the facts here to be explained?
> They are human communities, the family,

society and the state. Individualism has explained them--long ago. They are 'collections' held together by force, illusion or contract.[10]

But radical individualism is false. First it is historically false. Man has, so far as we know, always lived in communities. The Hobbesian state of nature never existed. There never was a time in history when individuals pursued their own selfish interests in a situation where there were no common social institutions, animated by a common morality. Second, the social behaviour of animals, and in particular primates from which humans evolved, indicates that human social groups, like animal social groups, are not mere collections of isolated individuals, but dynamic wholes which resemble living organisms more than machines.[11] An organic model, then, is more appropriate for understanding human communities than the mechanical models proposed by the radical individualists. Man is first a social being. So it makes no sense to argue, as radical individualism does, that the individual is ontologically independent of the social groups to which they belong. Third, radical individualism cannot explain the fact that the state claims rights over the individual which the ordinary citizen recognizes as legitimate. For example the state has the right to expropriate private property for the common good without the wish or consent of the owner. Proper compensation must be paid to the owner, but this does not rebut the state's claim. The state also has the right to make use of citizens themselves without their consent for the common good. It has the right to conscript people into the armed forces during national emergencies, and to suspend other individual rights.

People with virulent communicable diseases can be quarantined without their consent. These facts cannot be explained by any form of contract theory, since no individual contract was made with each individual citizen:

> . . . if we turn to practise, we find everywhere the state asserting itself as a power which had, and, if need be, asserts, the right to make use of and expend the property and person of the individual without regard to his wishes, and which, moreover, may destroy his life in punishment, and put forth other powers such as no theory of contract will explain except by the most palpable fictions, while at the same time no ordinary person calls their morality into question.[12]

The opposite hypothesis, institutionalism, which holds that the individual is ontologically dependent on social groups to which he belongs and social groups which are ontologically independent of the particular set of individuals which compose them, appears to be supported by the data. It is the social groups into which we are born, and which rear us, that determine the kind of person we develop into. It is the culture which moralizes the individual in the early stages of growth, particularly in stage two. It is only later, in stage three, that the individual begins to moralize the cultures he belongs to. If this evidence does not completely convince us of the truth of institutionalism and the falsity of radical individualism, Bradley suggests we try the following thought experiment. Think of any normal

Englishman you know and try to give an adequate account of who he is, without referring to the social groups into which he was born, and in which he grew up:

> Let us take a man, an Englishman as he is
> now, and try to point out that apart from
> what he has in common with others, apart
> from his sameness with others, he is not
> an Englishman--nor a man at all; that is,
> if you take him as something by himself,
> he is not what he is.[13]

Our personalities to some extent reflect our national character. We have uses for phrases like "a typical Scot," by which we mean a person who is dour, religious, canny, and overly sentimental about his native land. Or the "typical Canadian," by which we mean a person who is bland, businesslike, uncultured, but is good-natured and likes beer. Bradley develops his thesis in terms of the idea of national character, but it does not depend very heavily on the concept. Any social institution which plays a central role in personality formation would do equally well. The churches we attend, the schools which educate us, and especially the family, which plays the central role in the early development of personality. Bradley's central point is that you cannot understand any individual, including one's self, unless you understand that human personality is the product of the interaction between individuals and the communities which rear them:

> What we mean to say is, that he is what he
> is because he is a born and educated
> social being, and the member of an indi-
> vidual human organism; that if you make

> abstraction from all this, which is the
> same in him as in others, what you have
> left is not an Englishman or a man, but
> some I know not what residium, which never
> existed by itself and does not so exist.[14]

In short, we cannot understand who or what anyone
is, unless we look at them through the social institutions which helped create them. To understand any
person you must understand his biography, how this
particular individual came into being. Crispin Wright
has shown that Bradley's concept of the 'social organism'
is not a mere metaphor. He suggests, correctly, that if
all Bradley meant was that you cannot understand anyone
in abstraction from the society which reared them, then
few people would now dispute his claim. But he rightly
points out that Bradley means much more than this.[15] It
is important to stress that Bradley's position has a
clear ontological, as well as an epistemological, significance. He is saying that we would not be what we are if
it were not for the social groups which nurture us. The
individual is ontologically dependent on social institutions in this sense. Bradley does not imply that if
the particular groups to which someone is related were to
disappear, that the person would vanish:

> Of course we do not mean to say that he
> cannot go out of England without disap-
> pearing, nor, even if all the rest of the
> nation perished, that he would not sur-
> vive.[16]

Nor does Bradley mean that social groups can exist
independent of individuals. There are no social groups

which have no members. Bradley holds that social groups are concrete universals:

> Further, though universal, it is not
> abstract, since it belongs to its essence
> that is should be realized, and it has no
> real existence except in and through its
> particulars. The good will (for morality)
> is meaningless, if, whatever else it be,
> it be not the will of living finite
> beings.[17]

The universal has no existence independent of the particulars which give expression to it, or through which it expresses itself. There are no cultural traditions which exist outside the carriers of the tradition. Carriers of tradition are aware that they share in a social or communal process which has a history. The tradition existed before them, and if their efforts are successful, the tradition will exist after them. These traditions are expressed through social institutions and practises and membership in them defines our rights, freedoms and obligations. They define the ideals of the good teacher, the good doctor, the good son, the good parent and the good citizen, which we are expected to live up to. Of course, traditions die and new ones emerge, but these facts do not undermine Bradley's basic thesis. He is essentially correct in claiming that you cannot fully understand anyone, including oneself, apart from the cultures which in part produced them. It is impossible fully to analyze social groups in terms of sets of individuals who are merely externally related to one another. The relationship among individuals in a social group is internal or organic. You cannot fully understand a culture unless you understand its history, its traditions, social practices and institutions. A culture is itself a unique individual, which has a history and a structure, analogous to a person. The end product in both cases is a unique existence. The process of personality or societal formation is a process of individuation which produces a unique individual or society in every case. The psychological law of individuation which governs the process gives expression to the general ontological principle of internal relation, i.e., everything in the universe is interrelated and yet uniqueness is an essential characteristic of every aspect of existence:

> If the many are supposed to be without internal quality, each would forthwith become nothing, and we must therefore take each as being internally somewhat.[18]

The refutation of radical individualism is a variation of the metaphysical refutation of pluralism (the view that the universe consists of a number of independent reals which are externally related to each other, and can be or be understood independently of the relations they have to each other) Bradley developed in Appearance and Reality.[19] Bradley thinks that everything in the universe can only be fully understood, and fully be, in the light of, and because of, its internal relations to other reals. But this general principle does not deny individuality. Since all processes operate in terms of the principle, it is a way of understanding how individuals are created. Picasso once said: "What people forget is that everything is unique. Nature never produces the same thing twice,"[20] and that pretty well sums up Bradley's principle. The planets of the sun were all presumably produced by the same laws of nature but each is quite unique. And their uniqueness depends on the way they interacted with each other in the development of the solar system. So it is wrong to think of the law of individuation as a process which obliterates individuality. Rather it should be thought of as a law which explains how uniqueness and individuality develop. As Manser has demonstrated, for Bradley internal relations hold between particulars and not universals.[21]

This process of growth, we saw, goes through a series of distinct stages, and in some of these stages the individual identifies himself more fully with the society than in others. This is especially true of stage two, the stage of "My station and its duties." However the notion that morality consists entirely in conforming to existing moral codes is rejected as false by Bradley: "The sole root of morality consists in the direct identification of the individual will with the social will is false."[22] In stage two we saw that the society moralizes the private world of the individual, while in stage three the process is reversed. The private morality of the individual begins to alter the shape of public or social morality. The private world which emerges in stage three is not the amoral world of the Utilitarian or the lonely, unrealistic world of the moral loner, but a rich personal moral world which grows dialectically through our interpersonal and social relationships.

The problem in stage three is that morality appears to become coextensive with self-realization, and the pursuit of self-perfection. But this runs counter to our ordinary moral experience. It's true that we can realize ourselves by developing the virtues of intelligence and taste, but ordinary morality draws a clear distinction between the intellectual and the moral virtues. So all self-realization is not moral self-realization. Bradley accepts the distinction between moral and non-moral virtue, but argues that we have a moral duty to develop non-moral virtue. Bradley points out that we do give moral credit to anyone who develops into a good artist or a good scientist. We can distinguish different aspects of a person's life but this does not sanction chopping a person into several self-contained compartments which have no internal connection with each other. A person is a growing organic unity and so he/she cannot be said to be a moral being in one part of his/her life and an amoral being in another. The scientist is a moral being and you cannot separate his/her scientific from his/her moral life. In fact, if one tries to separate them, as we often try in the modern world, we create a dangerous and undesirable gap between morality and technology. Morality is intrinsically related to the growth of personality and so it will touch every aspect of our lives. Ideal morality must be personal as well as social:

> It is a moral duty to realize everywhere
> the best self, which for us in this sphere
> is an ideal self, and asking what morality
> is, we so far must answer it is co-
> extensive with self-realization in the
> self in and by me.[23]

The identification of morality and self-realization does appear to lead to at least three absurdities. First, it implies that every trifling detail of our lives would have to be approached with moral seriousness:

> If morality does not stop somewhere you
> must take it to be a moral question, not
> only whether a man amuses himself but also
> how he amuses himself. There will be no
> region of things indifferent and this
> leads to consequences absurd and immor-
> al.[24]

What difference does it make morally if I always tie
my left shoelace before I tie my right one? Or whether I
amuse myself on a Sunday afternoon by sitting in my
garden or going to a movie? If it is good to amuse
myself in ways which facilitate personal growth, and I do
not interfere with others, then the way I amuse myself is
surely morally indifferent. It is unreasonable to demand
that every aspect of our lives be considered from the
moral point of view. If we reject this then everything
we do would be a grave event. Lightness would vanish
from our lives and a somber moral earnestness would be
all pervasive.

Second, it implies that we have duties to the self
in precisely the same way as we have duties to others.
But as Kant recognized there is something paradoxical
about saying, "I have a duty to myself," because we
normally mean by an obligation a relationship that is
binding between at least two people. As Kant says: "If
the I who obligates is taken in the same sense as the I
who obligated, then the concept of a duty to oneself is
self-contradictory."[25] The idea of duty or obligation
implies that we have made some sort of contract with
another person. If I promise my friend I'll return the
money he loaned me in a week, then I've placed myself
under an obligation to return it in a week. If I don't
return the money to my friend when I said I would, my

friend has a right to demand it from me, or at least to expect an acceptable explanation from me for my failure to keep my promise. I should not be surprised if he were annoyed or angry with me, because that is his right also. But how can I put myself under an obligation to pay back money I borrow from myself? If I promise myself to return money I borrowed from myself on a certain day and fail to do so, how can I demand of myself that I fulfil the obligation? What sense does it make to claim a right against myself? Besides, only the promisee, the other party, can release me from an obligation before it is discharged. Since I can always release myself from the obligation whenever I please, there can be nothing truly binding in a duty to the self.

Third, it implies that society ought to take an interest in every aspect of our lives. The state has the right and the duty to enter the bedrooms of the nation. It denies the right to privacy along with most other individual rights. It leads or encourages the growth of totalitarian states and viciously paternalistic societies. Bradley thinks the first difficulty rests on a misunderstanding. He says:

> If it is my moral duty to go from one town
> to another, and there are two roads which
> are equally good, it is indifferent to the
> proposed moral duty which road to take, it
> is not indifferent that I do take one or
> the other; and whichever road I do take, I
> am doing my duty on it, and hence it is
> far from indifferent.[26]

Bradley's point can be put in another way. Duties of self-perfection are, as Kant recognized, imperfect

duties.[27] The obligation to perfect oneself in every way
does not imply a strict or precise set of duties. The
obligation allows for individual discretion. To perfect
oneself is a duty but precisely how this is to be done is
a matter of personal preference. Freedom is necessary
here because each moral agent is a unique individual.
Moral perfection is expressed individually.

The second difficulty, the paradox of duties to the
self, can be cleared up, according to Bradley, once we
recognize that our duties change, from social to personal
ones, when we pass from stage two to stage three. In
stage two, morality is seen primarily in terms of conformity to existing social codes. Duties are thought of as
being imposed upon us by society, hence all obligations
in this stage are duties required by others. In stage
two, duty is defined in utilitarian terms. To say, "X is
a duty" is to say, "we can be legitimately forced to do
or refrain from doing X." Stage two is the stage of law,
order and social control. In stage three the idea of
duty becomes personal. To be obliged means to act under
self-imposed moral laws. Stage three agents do their
duty because it is the right thing to do, and not because
they are forced to. It is reason, not fear, that binds a
stage three moral agent. Duties to self are not paradoxical if an obligation is seen as rationally binding. Not
only are duties to the self derived from reason, but
duties to others are as well. I am bound to keep my
promise and return the borrowed money to my friend even
if he has not the power to force me to do so. Only fully
rational moral agents can enter into stage three obligations with others. When they recognize duties to others
they are bringing their interpersonal and social relationships under the principle of individuation whose
objectives are richness and greater integration. When

they recognize duties to the self they are bringing their self-development under the same principle.

The third difficulty respecting excessive social control, paternalism, and totalitarianism is the most difficult for Bradley to deal with. It cannot be fully answered until we possess a completely developed idealist theory of rights. Bradley's draft for an idealist theory of rights is incomplete but it is sufficient to provide an initial answer to the problem.[28] For Bradley a right is a claim made on others to do, or refrain from doing, something. A right is a claim on others which is protected or enforced by law or custom. But enforcement is not always part of the definition or meaning of the concept of "a right":

> It is in order to secure the existence of rights in the acts of particular wills that compulsion is used. But compulsion is not necessary to the general or abstract definition of right, and it cannot be deduced from it.[29]

If the concept of 'a right' is tied logically to the idea of enforcement or social control, we would be unable to distinguish clearly between legal conventional and moral rights. Enforcement is certainly part of the definition of a legal or conventional right, because legal rights are enforced by law, and conventional rights by custom or institutional practice. But enforcement is not part of the definition or meaning of a moral right, or a morally justified claim on others. Legal and conventional rights are what Bradley calls real rights. They are rights which actually exist. They are rights which we actually have. Moral rights, on the other hand, are ideal rights. They are rights which do not exist but which ought to exist. They are rights which ought to be enforced:

> Wherever in the moral world you have law you also have right and rights. These may be real or ideal. The first are the will of the state or society, the second the will of the social-ideal or non-social ideal.[30]

Canadians, for example, have a legal right to refuse any medical treatment, including life-saving treatment. They have a conventional, but not a legal, right to death with dignity, because the right is recognized in the code of ethics of the Canadian Medical Association.[31] But they have neither a legal nor a conventional right to aid suicide. Physicians might under certain circumstances be legally allowed to stop treatment and let a patient die, but they cannot, under any circumstances, directly help them to die, even if the patient requests such help. Many Canadians believe that we have a moral right to aid suicide, i.e., we ought to have the legal right to aid suicide, if we are to take the right to death with dignity seriously. A right then cannot be fully justified unless it can be morally justified. Might is not right, and this is why Bradley thinks that all con-tractual theories cannot fully establish rights. They can at best establish legal or conventional rights, but neither legal nor conventional rights are fully justified unless they can be morally justified. As Bradley says:

> . . . they fail because their right is mere force, and is not moral, not right at

> all; and hence they can not show that I am
> in the right to obey it, or in the wrong
> to disobey it, but merely that, if I do
> not obey it, it may (or may not) be
> inconvenient for me.[32]

Moral rights give expression to the social ideal, the ideal of what a society ought to be. Real rights (legal and conventional rights) are the rights (duties/freedom) recognized in a stage two morality, the morality of "my station and its duties." Here rights are established by legitimate political authority or are recognized by custom in social groups or institutions. In stage one, the idea of a "right" is only primitively developed. If it exists at all, it would be what Hobbes called "the right of nature," the right to do whatever we please, including killing or harming others, in order to achieve our selfish ends:

> . . . everyone is governed by his own
> reason and there is nothing he can make
> use of that may not be a help unto him in
> preserving his life against his enemies--
> it follows that in such a condition every
> man has a right to everything, even to one
> another's body.[33]

Ideal or moral rights are the rights recognized in a stage three morality. Here rights are established by appeal to the principle of self-realization or self-perfection. For example the self-realization of an autonomous moral agent will require as much freedom from social control as is consistent with harmonious self-development:

. . . the progress of humanity being
furthered by the diversity of its elements, it is desirable in general that
individuals develop their nature. And
this shows there is a presumption against
extinction or hindrance of man or nation.[34]

An idealist theory of rights will include assent to
the principles of respect for persons, respect for life
and the principle of individual liberty, maximize individual human freedom as long as it doesn't interfere with
the self-development of others. Self-realization
requires freedom from social control but not freedom from
moral obligation. For Bradley freedom from social
control is not freedom to do as one pleases or moral
licence, but the psychological space each one of us needs
to grow morally:

It is almost as bad to have nothing but
duties as it is to have no duties at all.
For free individual self-development, we
must have both elements.[35]

The moral agent must be as free as possible to make
decisions about his life and death, and how he should
develop morally, intellectually, aesthetically, and
spiritually. The more freedom we have the greater our
personal moral responsibility becomes. A stage three
morality would still hold suicide to be immoral because
it is inconsistent with the principle of self-perfection
and the principle of respect for life. There is in a
stage three morality a presumption against the taking of
a human life. But Bradley does recognize that there are

exceptions to this rule, as there are to all moral rules. In fact dealing with exceptions to values we hold dear is, as we saw, a catalyst for moral growth. He points out that we make exceptions to the rule at both the personal and state level. Killing in self-defense or to protect the innocent is morally acceptable at the personal level. Capital punishment and killing in a just war are morally acceptable at the state level. Bradley thinks it is only Christian sentimentalism which leads us to hold that capital punishment is inhumane and morally wrong. For Bradley, life imprisonment is far more inhumane and cruel than capital punishment:

> To maintain in existence a creature, while depriving that creature of the conditions of happiness, is surely to inflict on it the direst suffering. Now, to pass such a sentence worse than death would, of course, be right if it were necessary and an ultimate resort. But in any other case it would be the extreme of indefensible cruelty.[36]

There is no absolute right to life for any individual, as some religious moralists argue. The idea that only God has the right to punish, or to use violence, is incoherent at best. For if violence is morally inappropriate for us then it should be inappropriate for God as well. Extreme pacifism denies the right of the state and the individual to use violence for the good of the individual or the common good. Both the individual and the state have, in the appropriate circumstances, the right to use violence to protect their interests.[37] Nor can an absolute right to life be derived by appeal to the secular doctrine of individual rights. It's not only that rights apart from community make no sense. An individual cannot grant himself/herself a right. But any set of rights derived from the doctrine of natural rights, or by contract, are bound to conflict. So there is no way within the theory of individual rights to resolve these conflicts:

> But the rights of these supposed individu-
> als, once placed in community, must
> necessarily collide, and all attempts to
> avoid this collision are idle. And to
> find a rational ground on which mutual
> interference is here legitimate, and there
> unlawful, is once more impossible.[38]

Mill's attempt, for example, to set up a single all encompassing principle from which a complete set of logically compatible individual rights could be deduced was doomed from the start.[39] There are no absolute rights. The general welfare, Bradley argues, is the proper goal of the state.[40] That goal and individual rights are bound to conflict and in certain cases the general welfare must take precedence over individual rights. Ensuring fair competition between competing individuals for economic goods is a role the state should perform. But not, Bradley argues, to the exclusion of helping the helpless, or of showing mercy to the helpless victims of competition:

> Mutual assistance, on the other hand,
> action in common, with more or less of
> self-sacrifice, is shown to be a condition
> of higher well-being.[41]

Justice will sometimes overrule benevolence but at
other times mercy will overrule justice. There is no way
of rationally predicting what will be the right course of
action to take. Whichever action, or policy, produces
the richest and most highly integrated state of affairs
will be right for that particular context. Whatever
allows the expression of both the conflicting values in
the least restricting way will be the right thing to do.
Even the principle of never punishing the innocent can be
overridden in certain circumstances, according to
Bradley:

> To remove the innocent is unjust, but it
> is not, perhaps, therefore in all cases
> wrong. Their removal on the contrary,
> will be right if the general welfare
> demands it. [42]

Bradley has in mind the case of the insane, incorrigible murderer. He/she is clearly innocent because
he/she is not willfully bad. They do what they do
because they are mentally ill. They are not then complete moral agents and so, like animals, are not the
proper object of punishment. The insane murder, then,
should be treated, not punished. But why, asks Bradley,
should the community give inviolable sanctity to the life
of a noxious lunatic? Doesn't the state have a duty to
protect its members from harm, as well as to secure their
liberty? Bradley says he is not advocating that society
apply capital punishment to insane murderers. To excise
the cancer from the moral organism, so to speak. He is
making a theoretical rather than a practical point. He
wants us to see both that there are no absolute rights
and that there is no abstract theoretical solution to the

problem of conflicting rights. As Peter Nicholson has pointed out, Bradley holds that political philosophy, like logic and ethics, is a theoretical subject which has only a limited application to practical politics.[43]

As noted before, there is a moral presumption against suicide in a stage three morality, but suicide can also be a genuine exception to the principle of sanctity of human life. In cases where the capacity for self-realization had been lost or is so severely diminished as to make life meaningless, suicide would be morally permissible. A stage three morality could also adopt a quite permissive legal attitude towards both suicide and aiding suicide. To maximize moral freedom it could support the legalization of both passive and active voluntary euthanasia. A legally permissive attitude towards suicide and aiding suicide combined with a more restrictive moral attitude towards them would maximize self-development and give fuller expression to the values of freedom and sanctity of human life. The idealist viewpoint allows the community to respect the needs of the terminally ill patient in a way which does not encourage disrespect for life, as the morally permissive position of the Utilitarian does, nor accept avoidable suffering as the Kantian position does. Bradley also thinks that active euthanasia is morally acceptable in certain situations: "Excusable killing is illustrated by the well-known story told in the Indian Mutiny of the husband who killed his wife."[44] In any case Bradley's idealism does not commit him to a totalitarian, or viciously paternalistic, society, as many of his interpreters, including Sidgwick, have claimed.[45]

Although the personal morality of stage three is clearly superior to the institutional morality of stage two, it is not free from problems. For one thing there is the conflict between duties to the self and duties to others, between private and public interest, between individual and state rights, between self-development and self-sacrifice. Bradley held that self-sacrifice was a fact of the moral life and a sound ethical theory had to be able to account for it. The problem is most serious for a stage three morality. In a stage two morality, self-sacrifice is real and easily justified. Right conduct in this stage means conformity to the moral rules in practice in the societies we dwell in. In fact, Bradley argues, all states require, in certain circumstances, individuals to sacrifice themselves for the good of the community:

> The sphere of private rights has rights only so long as it is right and is duty. It exists merely on sufferance; and the moment the right of the whole demands its suppression it has no rights. Public right everywhere overrides it in practise, if not in theory. This is the justification of such things as forceable expropriation, conscription, etc.[46]

In a stage two morality self-sacrifice is barely a real possibility. As Bradley indicates true self-sacrifice involves the real loss of personal good:

> It is self-sacrifice when I pursue an end by which my individuality suffers loss. In the attainment of this object my self is distracted or is diminished or even dissipated.[47]

But in stage two, the content of an individual's will is identical with that of his society, and his well-being is completely dependent on conforming to the morality in practice in his society. Total rebellion against society at this stage of moral development comes at a high psychological price. To reject society and its values is to repudiate part of oneself. The anguish of the rebel is the anguish of self-rejection. Here, society can and does require its individual members to make sacrifices for the good of the community. These sacrifices are seen as justified at this level of moral existence, and indeed individual rights are of little importance to the moral conformist. As Bradley says:

> He sees instincts are better and stronger than so-called 'principles.' He sees in the hour of need what are called 'rights' laughed at, 'freedom,' the liberty to do what one pleases, trampled on, the claims of the individual trodden under foot, and theories burst like cobwebs. And he sees, as of old, the heart of a nation rise high and beat in the breast of each one of her citizens, till her safety and her honour are dearer to each than life, till to those who live her shame and sorrow, if such is allotted, outweigh their loss, and death seems a little thing to those who go for her to their common and nameless grave.[48]

In stage two self-sacrifice, although real, is rarely a problem, because the agent can develop himself best by serving others, by self-sacrifice. In stage three, however, individual rights and the good of the individual must be taken seriously. Stage three is the stage where independent self-development becomes a true duty. It is here that the difficult conflict between duties to the self and duties to others, which involves genuine self-sacrifice, emerges:

> So far as they are discrepant, these two pursuits may be called, the one self-assertion, the other, self-sacrifice. And however much these must diverge, each is morally good; and, taken in the abstract, you cannot say that one is better than the other.[49]

A common mistake, according to Bradley, is to identify "self-assertion" with "living for others and not caring for the self." On this view morality is equated with selfless benevolence. To be virtuous means to benefit others and never the self. All virtue is seen as social virtue. But the view that morality is completely social, we have seen, is mistaken. Morality includes duties to the self, as well as duties to others. In fact, Bradley argues, in certain circumstances being virtuous requires neglecting others and looking after the self:

> . . . the neglect of social good, for the sake of pursuing other ends, may not only be moral self-assertion, but again, equally under other conditions, it may be moral sacrifice. We can even say that 'living for others' rather than living

'for myself,' may be immoral and self-ish.[50]

Conflicts between duties to the self and duties to others are resolved in stage three by the principle of individuation. If acting in the interests of others produces self-growth, creates a richer, more integrated personality, then it is right to act in the interests of others. If the opposite is true, then it is right to act in one's own interest. Bradley believes that generally there is no conflict between duties to the self and duties to others. The interests of society and the individual usually coincide:

> The whole is furthered most by the self-seeking of its parts, for in these alone the whole can appear and be real. And the part again is individually bettered by its action for the whole, since thus it gains the supply of that common substance which is necessary to fill it.[51]

Bradley holds that competition within a system of justice (fairness) is required for the good of society:

> The good of the whole is the end, and competition of the individual is a means, for if the best do not come to the front there is general loss. And so the community sanctions self-assertion, and it lays down the limits and conditions of self-seeking. You may not kill or steal, but you may struggle against one another for existence.[52]

Competitiveness is a personal as well as a social virtue. It is necessary for self-development. To grow we need to develop self-respect and self-confidence. To do this we need to test ourselves in fair competition against others. Aggressive self-assertion is morally acceptable so long as we compete within the rules of justice: "Selfishness is not wicked, for the state encourages its citizens to be selfish, and violence is not wicked, for the state is violent towards its citizens."[53] There is, then, a general harmony between the good of the society and the good of the individual. Bradley believed, however, that both unlimited self-sacrifice and unlimited self-assertion are contrary to sound morality. Self-assertion needs to be limited because although it may be good for the society as a whole, it is not always good for every individual member of the society. Take economic competition, for example:

> But even if competition in trade is ultimately for the good of humanity, it is hard to believe that the advantage must come to every man. Men and nations take time to find the better trade they have been compelled to seek. They suffer in the process and they do not always survive it and while their competition is gaining, he surely sometimes must gain what they lose, and after all has sought his own at the expense of his neighbour.[54]

Thus within limits, self-assertion is desirable, and the important question now becomes, as J. S. Mill saw, "what are the legitimate limits of social control?"[55] In stage two morality these limits would be the rules of justice and fairness in practice in a particular society. In a stage three morality these rules would be established by the idealist principle of liberty: "Do whatever is necessary to realize yourself, so long as you do not interfere with the self-realization of others." A stage three morality will be able to resolve the conflict between duties to the self and duties to others more adequately than the morality of earlier stages. Still it will not be able, according to Bradley, to achieve the perfect harmony between the self and others which morality demands. The reason for this is that even if we are operating at a personal level, which is well aware of the limits of institutional morality, we still require society to grow: "But we have found that the very essence of finite beings is self-contradictory, that their own nature includes relation to others, and that they are already each outside of its own existence."[56] The needs of the self and the needs of society often coincide so that self-assertion will also advance the interests of others, and helping others realize themselves helps us to realize ourselves. But this seems not always the case. Bradley is still pessimistic about the legitimate claims society still has on us. In a perfect society there would be no requirement for self-sacrifice, for in it everyone's needs would be met. But we do not live in perfect societies, nor in a perfect world. As Bradley says: "No existing social organism secures to its individuals any more than an imperfect good, and in all of them self-sacrifice marks the fact of a failure in principle."[57] The problem is that institutions are a prerequisite for personal growth. We all need societies of some sort, even imperfect ones, in order to develop. And imperfect societies, because of their nature, require sacrifices. These sacrifices cannot be understood by a stage three morality because they are inconsistent with the principle of self-realization. No one can be required to sacrifice his/her life for others, because premature death cuts short self-realization. This obligation clearly goes beyond what can be required of any individual by any society. We have reached the sphere of the supererogatory which transcends our finite moralities. This is the world of heroes and saints, which represents a higher but not purely moral stage of development. We have arrived at stage four, at religious morality. The sacrifices which the saint or hero makes are seen by them as duties. The obligations are real, and legitimate, they are facts in the moral world, but they cannot be explained at the level of morality alone. We need to move to stage four, to the level of religious morality, to come to terms with the conflict our finitude creates:

> Morality in brief calls for an unattain-
> able unity of its aspects, and in its
> search for this, it naturally is led
> beyond itself into a higher form of
> goodness. It ends in what we may call
> religion.[58]

The moral consciousness must be absorbed into the religious consciousness at this level of self-development. For the moral consciousness, evil of any kind is undesirable. Whether it be pain, frustration, immorality or self-sacrifice. At stage three we have a duty to try to get rid of evil: ". . . from the moral point of view, evil and with it self-sacrificing virtue are both undesirable; we must look at them as things which ought not to be."[59] But this implies that a universe free of evil, suffering, and pain, would be a better universe than one which included them. But is this true? What reasons do we have for believing this? Bradley thinks that our moral experience suggests however dimly that the opposite might be true. Evil we saw, although not on a par with good, is still a necessary part of the moral process:

> In our moral experience we find this whole fact given beyond question. We suffer within ourselves a contest of the good and the bad wills and a certainty of evil. Nay, if we please, we may add that this dischord is necessary, since without it morality must wholly perish.[60]

The conflict between good and evil is necessary for morality to exist. Yet the goal of the process is to rid the universe of evil. So if morality succeeds it will annihilate itself. The process of morality is self-transcending. In the end, whether we are aware of it or not, we as moral agents desire to become non-moral, to develop beyond the struggle of good and evil, to a higher level of existence which is again richer and more fully integrated: "For morality desires unconsciously, with the suppression of evil, to become wholly non-moral.[61]

To claim that a universe free of evil is better than a world which includes it is to claim that a universe without moral agents would be better than a world which contains them. This is a paradox which exists in a stage three morality but not in a stage four morality. At stage four all life, indeed the whole of existence, is seen as sacred. Everything in the universe possess value, including the moral struggle which characterizes the life of the moral agent. This does not imply that we have no duty to try to rid the universe of evil. To be moral in a stage three sense is also a religious duty. But it does mean that our attitude towards existence as a whole has changed. For example, in stage four everyone is considered to be equally valuable. According to Bradley the principle of absolute equality is a religious rather than a purely moral principle. "There is a sense in which all men have equal and incomparable value but that sense falls outside morality."[62] For morality all men are not of equal value. In this world some men are better than others. Hence the principle of respect for human life is not primary. We have a right to defend ourselves from the evil of others, and a duty to protect the innocent. We are not required to turn the other cheek. Pacifism is not a defensible moral stance. We have a right to use as much violence as necessary to protect ourselves and the innocent:

> Universal love doubtless is a virtue but tameness and baseness--to turn the cheek to every rascal who smites it, to suffer the robbery of villains and the contumely of the oppressor, to stand by idle when the helpless are violated and the land of one's birth in its death struggle, and to leave honour and vengeance and justice to God above--are qualities that deserve some other epithet.[63]

In certain cases we might have to take a life to save an innocent one which is threatened. Morally we are only allowed to use as much force as is necessary to achieve the desired good. Excessive use of force or violence is immoral. Still in some circumstances to take another's life is the morally right thing to do. Bradley, as we saw, thought that capital punishment might be morally justified: ". . . if we take the case of criminals, or savages without the community, it surely may be right to abolish their existence."[64] War can also be justified morally within a stage three morality. Bradley believes in the just war. He argues that war is not illegal because there does not exist an international law backed up by a legitimate world government. And even if there was an effective world government, it would have to use force to establish its law. Pacifism at the international level is as self-contradictory as at the national or personal level, because it denies us the right to use force to protect national and individual rights: "The meek will not inherit the earth, and a nation which claims morality must be ready to use force in defense of right."[65]

Accepting a stage four perspective would not, according to Bradley, have much direct effect on the substance of morality. The content would be much the same, though the spirit in which it is done would be different. Changes in conduct would be indirect and subtle. For one thing our attitude towards immorality would change. We would exercise more caution with judgements of personal blame. Immorality would become sin, and punishment, attonement. To treat the sinner in ways which would impede self-development would always be wrong. There would be a general shift from justice towards compassion, charity and forgiveness of others. Capital punishment and war would become less appealing because the principle of sanctity of life would be more dominant. We would also be inclined to incorporate the whole of nature within the community of things which possess intrinsic value.

In stage one animals and nature would possess only instrumental value. They would be used, like everything else, as a means to the gratification of the agent's appetites. In stage two, animals and nature would still not be part of the moral community. They would be used, however, to further the moral as well as the material well-being of the agent. Wanton cruelty to animals and wanton destruction of nature would be frowned on by society because of the bad moral influence such behaviour would have on the developing moral agent. Someone who pulls the wings off flies for amusement is likely to be just as cruel to human beings in the future. In stage three animals and nature begin to be integrated into the moral community. In this stage the moral community has been expanded to include the whole of humanity. This expansion would involve the recognition that we have obligations to future, as well as present generations, hence the natural environment would become an important moral concern. We would have an obligation to see that the natural environment was as good as when we inherited it. It is only a short step from this view to recognizing that animals and nature possess intrinsic value and so belong to the moral community. Bradley doesn't think it makes much sense to talk of the rights of animals or nature, although it does make sense to talk of direct obligations to them. To have a right we must be able to recognize the duties which go with the right. Neither nature nor animals have this capacity:

> . . . inanimate matter would have rights, e.g., the very dirt in the road would 'have a right' to be taken up or let lie--and this is barbarous.[66]

Nevertheless both animals and nature, because they are intrinsically valuable, are the direct objects of duty: "Has a beast rights? He is the object of duties, not the subject of rights."[67] Towards the end of stage three the moral community has been expanded to include not only the whole of sentient creation but the whole of creation. Everything in the universe now possesses value. Stage three has developed into stage four. Religious morality, for Bradley, is fundamentally personal. It is an attitude of mind and not the mere observance of ritual. It is a development of the personal, rather than the social, side of morality. Personal virtue in stage four would shift towards humility and away from vanity; towards hope in the ultimate goodness of the universe, and faith in the ultimate coherence of existence. In this stage we try to come to terms with our finitude. But like the previous stages of moral development stage four also has its internal stresses, which impel the religious moral agent to a final mystical union with existence as a whole.

The development of the religious consciousness like the moral consciousness is a process which passes through stages which define the relationship between man and his god(s):

> Religion is therefore a process with inseparable factors, each appearing on either side. It is the unity of man and God, which in various stages and forms wills, and knows itself throughout.[68]

Religion like morality is a process, and all processes are inherently contradictory. The goal of the religious consciousness is the mystical union of man with

God. If the goal of religion is achieved then man, his religion, and his God(s) would vanish:

> . . . the effort of religion is to put an end to, and break down, this relation--a relation which, none the less, it essentially presupposes. Hence, short of the absolute, God cannot rest, and having reached that goal he is lost, and religion with him. [69]

The end of the moral journey is a mystical union between God and man, in which the distinction, but not the difference, between them has vanished. They exist as one harmonious whole in which there is diversity but no relations, in which there is richness of feeling but no desire, for all desire has been satisfied. The end of the journey is very much like it's beginning. The line has returned into itself and become a circle.

NOTES

CHAPTER VI: PERSONAL AND SOCIAL MORALITY

1   F. H. Bradley, Ethical Studies, p. 164.
2   J. S. Mill, Utilitarianism: Collected Works, Vol. X., p. 246. For a utilitarian analysis of suicide, see D. Hume, "Suicide," in Of the Standard of Taste, Liberal Arts, 1965, pp. 151-160, and R. Brandt, "The Morality and Rationality of Suicide," in Moral Problems, Harper & Row (third edition), 1979, pp. 460-489.
3   Kant, Ethical Philosophy (The Metaphysics of Morals), p. 21.
4   Kant, The Critique of Pure Reason (translated by Norman Kemp Smith) (MacMillan, 1933), p. 312.
5   Hobbes, Leviathan (Liberal Arts, 1958), p. 106.
6   Kant, Ethical Philosophy (The Metaphysics of Morals), p. 83.
7   Kant, Ibid., p. 78. The brackets are mine.
8   F. H. Bradley, Appearance and Reality, p. 382.
9   F. H. Bradley, Ethical Studies, p. 178.
10 F. H. Bradley, Ibid., p. 164.
11 F. H. Bradley, Ibid., pp. 163-174.
12 F. H. Bradley, Ibid., pp. 164-165, cf. p. 212, and "Some Remarks on Punishment," Collected Essays, p. 150.
13 F. H. Bradley, Ibid., p. 166.
14 F. H. Bradley, Ibid., p. 166.
15 Crispin Wright, "The Moral Organism," The Philosophy of F. H. Bradley, (Manser and Stich), pp. 82-83.
16 F. H. Bradley, Ibid., p. 166.
17 F. H. Bradley, Ibid., p. 162.
18 F. H. Bradley, Appearance and Reality, p. 124.

19   F. H. Bradley, Ibid., pp. 124-126.

20   Pablo Picasso (Quoted in Françoise Gilot and Carlton Lake), Life With Picasso, (McGraw Hill, 1964), Signet, 1965, p. 51.

21   A Manser, Bradley's Logic, pp. 122-123.

22   F. H. Bradley, Appearance and Reality, p. 381.

23   F. H. Bradley, Ethical Studies, p. 219.

24   F. H. Bradley, Ibid., p. 216.

25   Kant, Ethical Philosophy (The Metaphysics of Morals), p. 77.

26   F. H. Bradley, Ethical Studies, p. 216.

27   Kant, Ethical Philosophy (The Metaphysics of Morals), pp. 89-91.

28   F. H. Bradley, "Rights and Duties," Notes to Essay V, Ethical Studies, pp. 207-213.

29   F. H. Bradley, Ibid., p. 208.

30   F. H. Bradley, Ibid., p. 208.

31   See Patients' Rights in Ontario, Toronto, 1982, p. 11, or Rosovsky, The Canadian Patients' Book of Rights (Doubleday, Toronto, 1980).

32   F. H. Bradley, Ethical Studies, p. 209.

33   Hobbes, Leviathan, p. 110.

34   F. H. Bradley, "The Limits of Individual and National Self-Sacrifice," Collected Essays, pp. 168-169.

35   F. H. Bradley, Ethical Studies, p. 210.

36   F. H. Bradley, "Some Remarks on Punishment," Collected Essays, p. 161.

37   F. H. Bradley, Ibid., p. 157.

38   F. H. Bradley, Ibid., p. 158.

39   J. S. Mill, "On Liberty," The Collected Works of John Stuart Mill, Vol. XVIII, pp. 223-224.

        Mill, of course was neither a natural rights theorist nor a contract theorist. He relied solely on the principle of utility as the

　　　　　foundation of ethics and politics. The re-
　　　　　sults, however, from Bradley's point of view,
　　　　　were the same. Cf. pp. 224-225.

40　F. H. Bradley, "Some Remarks on Punishment," Col-
　　lected Essays, p. 152.

41　F. H. Bradley, Ibid., p. 160.

42　F. H. Bradley, Ibid., p. 155.

43　Peter Nicholson, "Bradley as a Political Philoso-
　　pher," The Philosophy of F. H. Bradley (Manser and
　　Stock), pp. 119-121.

44　F. H. Bradley, Ethical Studies, p. 158 (footnote 1).

45　Cf. P. Nicholson, "Bradley as a Political Philoso-
　　pher," p. 117ff.

46　F. H. Bradley, Ethical Studies, p. 212.

47　F. H. Bradley, Appearance and Reality, p. 369.

48　F. H. Bradley, Ethical Studies, p. 184.

49　F. H. Bradley, Appearance and Reality, p. 367.

50　F. H. Bradley, Ibid., p. 368.

51　F. H. Bradley, Ibid., p. 370.

52　F. H. Bradley, Collected Essays, p. 171.

53　F. H. Bradley, Ibid., p. 172.

54　F. H. Bradley, Ibid., p. 172.

55　J. S. Mill, "On Liberty," Collected Works,
　　Vol. XVIII, p. 217.

56　F. H. Bradley, Appearance and Reality, p. 370.

57　F. H. Bradley, Ibid., p. 373.

58　F. H. Bradley, Ibid., p. 388.

59　F. H. Bradley, Collected Essays, p. 131.

60　F. H. Bradley, Appearance and Reality, p. 178.

61　F. H. Bradley, Ibid., p. 178.

62　F. H. Bradley, Collected Essays, p. 168.

63　F. H. Bradley, Ibid., p. 173.

64　F. H. Bradley, Ibid., p. 168.

65　F. H. Bradley, p. 176.

66   F. H. Bradley, Ethical Studies, p. 207.

67   F. H. Bradley, Ibid., p. 208.

68   F. H. Bradley, Appearance and Reality, p. 394.

69   F. H. Bradley, Ibid., pp. 395-396.

APPENDIX

BRADLEY'S STAGES OF THE MORAL LIFE

(1) Stage One: Egotistical Hedonism

- Child is essentially concerned with the hedonistic consequences of particular actions for itself (Proto-Utilitarianism).
- Child's thinking is instrumental, concrete, particular and categorical.
- Learning process is one of trial and error. Rules are simple generalizations from experience.
- Reason is the slave of the passions.
- Selfishness predominates, others, animals, and nature have only instrumental value.
- Simple appetite is the basic emotional structure for the child.

(2) Stage Two: Institutionalism

- Child acts in accordance with the rules of the social groups to which he/she belongs; the family, peer groups, churches, schools and the state.
- Child's thinking is symbolic, abstract, universal and hypothetical.
- Thought is theoretical as well as practical and is no longer the slave of the passions.
- Moral thinking is essentially non-consequentialist. Rightness or wrongness are determined by conformity/non-conformity to moral rules (Proto-Kantian). Morality is also conventional, conformist and relativistic. (Proto-Idealistic).

- Desire replaces appetite as the basic emotional structure in the child.
- The good and the bad self appear and moral education begins.
- Legal and conventional rights are recognized.
- Animals and nature are now objects of indirect duties.
- The social virtues of obedience, justice, and, to a lesser extent, benevolence predominate.
- The moral community includes members of the social groups to which the child belongs.

(3) Stage Three: Personalism
- Morality becomes critical and personal.
- Thought becomes critical and systematic.
- The moral agent thinks in terms of a growing system of universal moral principles (e.g., the principle of respect for persons, beneficence, non-maleficence, fairness and self-perfection). The moral community is extended to include the whole of humanity.
- The child is now a fully developed moral agent; a self-legislating moral being who strives to harmonize thought, emotion, and conduct into a system which is as rich and integrated as possible.
- The principle of individuation becomes the conscious standard for morality.
- Rights become ideal (moral) based on the principle of self-realization.
- Animals and nature become direct objects of duty.
- The personal virtues, as well as the social virtues, are developed.

(4)   Stage Four: Religious-Mystical

- Morality develops beyond itself (beyond moral good and evil) to a mystical/religious metaphysical perspective.
- Thought incorporates faith as well as reason.
- The fundamental moral attitude is that existence is sacred.
- The religious moral agent tries to come to terms with human finitude.
- The religious moral agent recognizes that all animals, plants and nature possesses intrinsic value and he/she tries to incorporate this into a coherent system of thought, feeling, and action.
- The supererogatory virtues of heroic self-sacrifice, faith, hope and charity are developed.

INDEX

168; criterion of truth 35; criticism of formal logic 27; criticism of Kant's ethics 86, 87, 92; criticism of moral skepticism 42; criticism of metaphysical and moral skepticism are sound 44; criticism of the syllogism (39, note 43; on cruelty 136, 137, 138; and deductive reasoning 21; defense of principle of self-realization not inductive or deductive 36; on desire 124, 125, 129, 130, and determinism 54; and developmental psychology 148; dialecting between moral rates and particular moral experience 102; on diminished responsibility 107; on discord and morality 236, on distinction between animal and human intelligence 153; distinction between practical and theoretical ethics 29; on the distinction between psychological idealism and psychological egoism 113; distinguishes ideal and real rights 222; distinguishes moral and non-moral virtues 217; does not commit the naturalistic fallacy 36; on duty 219, 224; on economic competition 226; on emotion (198, note 75); on emotion in moral development 182; on ethical theory and practical ethics 98; on

ethics 147; on ethics and morality 97; on ethics and psychology 42; ethics not based on religion 173; on evil 138, 139, 180, 236; on exceptions to moral rules 224, 225; and experimental methodology 186; on faith 178; and false models of reasoning 23; final proofs are metaphysical 20; on formal ethics 92; on free self-development 224; on general welfare as goal of state 226; on goal of ethical theory 184, 185; on good 138; on goodness and evil 135; on goodness as realization of perfection 140; on hedonism 75; on higher and lower pleasures 73, 74, 75; on ideal and real rights 221; and ideal experiments 24; and the idealist theory of rights 221; importance of (preface, 4); on the impossibility of pure malevolence 135; and inductive reasoning 23; on internal relations 216; on interpersonal relationships and growth 138; on intuitive understanding in moral reasoning 185; on just war 225, 238; and Kantian and utilitarian sociologies 200; on Kantianism and facts of moral experience 108; on Kant's ethics 85, 93; on Kant's formalism 84; on Kant's psychology 82; on Kant's use of moral rules 94; on Kant's view

STUDIES IN THE HISTORY OF PHILOSOPHY